CLASSIC TUNES & TALES

Ready-to-Use Music Listening Lessons & Activities for Grades K-8

TOD F. KLINE

Artwork by Toya B. Warner

PARKER PUBLISHING COMPANY
West Nyack, New York 10994

Library of Congress Cataloging-in-Publication Data

Kline, Tod F.
    Classic tunes & tales : ready-to-use music listening lessons
& activities for K-8 / Tod F. Kline ; [artwork by Toya B. Warner].
        p.   cm.
    ISBN 0-13-762683-5
    1. Music appreciation—Study and teaching (Elementary)—Activity
programs. I. Title.
MT10.K55 1997
372.87'2—dc21
                                                      97-27577
                                                         CIP
                                                        MN

Printed in the United States of America

10 9 8 7 6 5 4 3 2 1

ISBN 0-13-762683-5

PARKER PUBLISHING COMPANY
West Nyack, NY 10994

A Simon & Schuster Company

On the World Wide Web at http://www.phdirect.com

Prentice Hall International (UK) Limited, *London*
Prentice Hall of Australia Pty. Limited, *Sydney*
Prentice Hall Canada, Inc., *Toronto*
Prentice Hall Hispanoamericana, S.A., *Mexico*
Prentice Hall of India Private Limited, *New Delhi*
Prentice Hall of Japan, Inc., *Tokyo*
Simon & Schuster Asia Pte. Ltd., *Singapore*
Editora Prentice-Hall do Brasil, Ltda., *Rio de Janeiro*

About *Classic Tunes & Tales*

This practical resource gives elementary music teachers a unique collection of short, stimulating, easy-to-use lessons and activities to develop students' interest in classical music while building their knowledge of the basic elements of music. The "classic tunes and tales" in the lessons appeal to children because they feature short, interesting stories, catchy tunes, and easy-to-learn words and music. The tunes are popular melodies selected from the works of the greatest composers in history. The tales are stories about composers, operas and ballets. And the words accompanying each tune help students remember facts about the music and the composer.

You will find these tunes and tales appropriate for most elementary and middle school students, though each situation must be considered to assure success. Each tune and tale must also be delivered by the teacher with enthusiasm and joy. Memorization of the stories is suggested for more effective dramatization. Pictures, props, or skits can be used to reinforce and motivate while involving students.

The tunes and tales may be taught in a short, 3-to-10-minute segment of a class, followed by the lesson activities. Many of these classics have been heard by kids on television, in movies, and elsewhere—so it is crucial that we relate them to what is familiar to children. It is also essential to review learned tunes, assuring that students maintain and absorb each one.

For easy use, the 50 tunes and 50 tales in this resource are organized into five sections, or levels, with suggested grades for use, though all materials can be readily adapted for higher or lower levels. The first page of each section lists the tunes in that section along with the music element and concept stressed with a particular tune, for example, "Minuet" (Rhythm, Meter in 3). Each lesson focuses on one classic piece and its composer and includes the following components:

> **Lesson Plan Page:** The lesson plan spells out the specific lesson objective, materials needed for the lesson, and step-by-step procedures for presenting the classic tune and story, teaching the music, and using two or more related activities.
>
> **Story Page:** The story page provides interesting background information about the music and/or its composer to be read aloud by the teacher. This can also be copied for the students.
>
> **Music Page:** The music page presents a catchy musical excerpt from the classic tune along with words related to the tune and the composer to help students remember both.
>
> **Activity Page:** The accompanying page(s) offer one or more reproducible activity sheets, games, or puzzles to reinforce the lesson, ready to be photocopied as many times as you need them for use with individual students or an entire class.

A special "Supplementary Materials" section at the end of the book is packed with a variety of related materials, to be used as you deem appropriate. These include eight brief classic tune selections for recorder, games and reproducible puzzles for reviewing composer facts and music terms and symbols, and a "Classic Tunes & Tales Historical Timeline" that will help students relate composers and their works to major events at the time, such as the invention of the printing press or the Declaration of Independence. You will also find eight simple bulletin board plans with sample display diagrams for topics such as "Symbols in Music," "Music Taking Form," and "Composers Around the World."

Each of the five sections, or levels, of musical experience in this resource ends with some type of reproducible quiz or exam to evaluate students' retention of the new material. The tunes may be played on the piano or a recording of the original. However, consider progressing slowly to the original if you teach the tunes on the piano.

Classic Tunes & Tales is meant to give you a store of ready-to-use music appreciation lessons and activities to supplement and enrich your music program. It is hoped that these will encourage you to compose and arrange other masterworks in the effort to promote and develop your students' interest in the great classics.

Tod F. Kline

Dedication

To my wife, family, and the students of the Waynesboro
Area School District.

Contents

LEVEL II
(Grade Levels: 2–3)
53

LEVEL III
(Grade Levels 3–4)
115

**LEVEL IV
(Grade Levels 4–8)
169**

LEVEL V
(Grade Levels 5–8)
231

SUPPLEMENTARY MATERIALS
313

LEVEL I:
(GRADE LEVELS: K-2)

William Tell Overture
(ROSSINI)

Lesson Plan

Objective: Students will identify and recognize the *William Tell Overture* theme and story.

Materials: Piano
Copies of the Story Sequence Activity Page
Copies of the Story Sequence Cut-Outs
Glue
Scissors
Props (if you plan to go all the way and act out the story)

Procedure: 1. **Tell the story** of William Tell to the students by acting it out through motions, expressions, props, and exaggerations.

2. **Define** an overture: the opening or beginning music to a program or show.

3. **Teach the tune** to the students. First, the words phrase by phrase. Second, the music phrase by phrase.

4. **Activity:** Have the students act out the story. Choose students to be William Tell, the son, the king, village people, and the king's guards.

Have the village people walk by and bow to the hat as it is being guarded. Tell and his son walk by the hat without bowing, defying the king's law. The guards escort Tell to prison. The king makes a deal with Tell. Tell's son is placed at a tree with an apple on his head. By miming, Tell pulls out an arrow and places it on the bow. He fires and misses. He prepares another imaginary arrow. He shoots it and it is a good shot. The crowd cheers. Tell and his son walk off leaving the village.

Activity Page: Use the story sequence to help the students remember the story. Have the students place the cutout that corresponds with the proper place and order in the story as it occurs.

Story of William Tell

Once upon a time there was an archery marksman named William Tell who traveled throughout the European countryside with his son hunting and perfecting his archery skills.

One day Tell and his son journeyed into a village ruled by an eccentric king. As they walked through the village, they passed by a tall pole with a hat on top of it. They noticed people bowing in respect to it as each one walked by. William Tell felt this was silly, so he ignored the hat and moved on. As Tell passed it, people were shocked and astonished to see that this hunter would do such a thing. Shortly, the king's guardsmen arrived, and they escorted William Tell off to prison.

The reason for William Tell's imprisonment was that he had broken the king's law that states "everyone who passes the hat must bow to it"; the king adored this hat so much he felt everyone should honor it.

After a few days, everyone realized that William Tell had a son who needed to be taken care of, so the king offered Tell a proposition (deal) to earn his freedom. The king said that William Tell would be freed if he could shoot an apple off his son's head with an arrow. Mr. Tell, being an expert marksman, decided to try. He was allotted only two arrows, so was given only two tries. So his son was placed at a tree with an apple on his head. Mr. Tell fitted the first arrow, aimed, and fired. It went wide. He fitted the next and last arrow, keenly aimed, and fired. Bullseye! It was a perfect shot. The king kept his word, and William Tell was freed. He and his son moved on, traveling throughout the countryside.

Musical Excerpt
from the *William Tell Overture*
GIACCHINO ROSSINI (1792–1868)

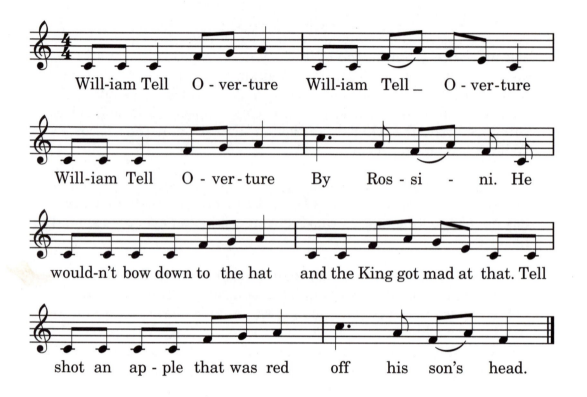

Name _____

Story Sequence Activity Page

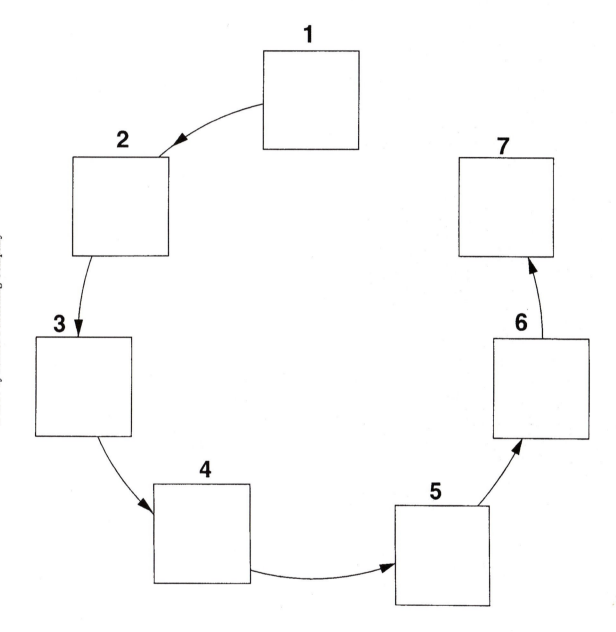

Story Sequence Cut-Outs

Eine Kleine Nacht Musik
(MOZART)

Lesson Plan

Objective: Students will learn to recognize fast, happy, and lively music.

Materials: Piano
Listening Examples of Fast/Slow
Listening Examples of Sad/Happy
Copies of the Tempo & Mood Listening Activity Page
Pencils or crayons

Procedure:
1. ***Tell the story*** of *Eine Kleine Nacht Musik* to the students. Translate the title. Explain that a serenade is music intended for the evening.

2. ***Play the tune***. Ask the students if the tune is slow or fast. Also, ask if it is sad or happy.

3. ***Teach the tune*** to the students. Remember to teach the words first, then the tune—phrase by phrase.

4. ***Activity:*** Play examples of slow and fast music. Have the students walk for slow and run for fast. Be sure to remind them to stay in their own space. Next, play examples of sad and examples of happy music. Have the students mimic crying for sad and to exaggerate a smile for happy.

5. ***Activity:*** Ask the students to name words or things that are fast, lively, and happy. Follow up by asking for songs they may know that are fast, happy, and lively. A great reinforcement is to play a few of the songs and have them sing and move around the room in a circle as a class. Skip, jump, hop, jog, clap, or whatever may be appropriate. Example: "If You're Happy And You Know It."

Activity Page: The students must circle the pictures that best describe the speed and mood of Mozart's serenade.

Story of *Eine Kleine Nacht Musik*

Eine Kleine Nacht Musik is German. In English it means "a little night music." Mozart composed it in one day back in 1787 (around the time of George Washington and Ben Franklin). It is a serenade. A serenade is music intended for festive evening social occasions. This work probably stands between chamber music (music performed by a small group in a chamber or a room) and orchestral music (music performed by a large group in an auditorium or large area). It's been said that Mozart kept this music in his head for months while he was ill until he finally was able to write it down.

Mozart was well known for composing music in his head at any place and any hour, so much so, he would think, work, and play quite vigorously. Once, he decided to take up the game of billiards for fun and relaxation. But he began to spend hours upon hours playing billiards, so he really wasn't getting much rest and relaxation. Those people who played billiards with him felt that the reason he played for such long periods of time was because he was composing the music of an opera in his head while he played.

Musical Excerpt
from *Eine Kleine Nacht Musik*
WOLFGANG AMADEUS MOZART
(1756–1791)

9

Listening Examples of Fast/Slow

America

Chicken Scratch

Oh, Suzanna

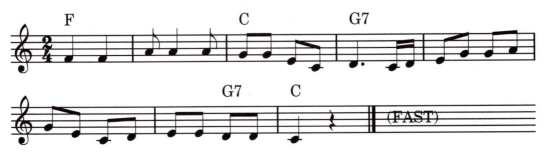

Row, Row, Row Your Boat

Listening Examples of Sad/Happy

When You're Happy

Volga Boatman

Still Raining

Shoo Fly

Cock Robin

Jimmy Crack Corn

Tempo & Mood
Listening Activity Page

Speed of Music (Tempo)

Mood of Music

The Surprise Symphony
(HAYDN)

Lesson Plan

Objective: Students will recognize and perform the long and short rhythms
(♩ , ♩)

Materials: Piano
Copies of the Count & Play Rhythm Activity Page
Pencils or crayons

Procedure: 1. **Tell the story** to the students.

2. **Teach the tune** to the students.

3. **Focus the lesson** on rhythm. Have the students tap their legs
for ♩ and tap and slide for ♩. Tap along with the students. Do a
variety of rhythms:

4. **Activity:** Using rhythm sticks or clapping, allow students to create their own long-short rhythms. Possibly, have the others echo
the brief rhythms. The teacher should echo the rhythm first, in
order to clean up any miscommunication of rhythms.

Activity Page: Rhythm Activity Page:

a. Tap along—have the students tap along as you play the tune.
Tap for (Z) and tap slide for (Z__).

b. Say and play—have the students say the words or the rhythm
syllables while tapping along. Tah (♩) and Tah-ah (♩).

Story of *The "Surprise" Symphony*

Papa Haydn, as Franz Josef Haydn was nicknamed, was one of many composers who worked for royal or political leaders in order to earn a living. He composed many symphonies for his boss, the prince. The prince was very fond of Haydn's music for instruments only (instrumental music), especially his fast and lively pieces. However, on some evenings, the prince would attend a concert by Haydn after eating a big meal. The concerts were sometimes quite lengthy, so the prince occasionally dozed off during the program.

This perturbed Haydn, so he was determined to do something about it. Haydn's solution was to compose a symphony which would contain a section quiet enough to put the prince to sleep. Once he drifted off, a loud unexpected chord of music would be played to startle and awaken those who dared to fall asleep during Maestro Haydn's concert!

Musical Excerpt
from *The "Surprise" Symphony*
FRANZ JOSEF HAYDN (1732–1809)

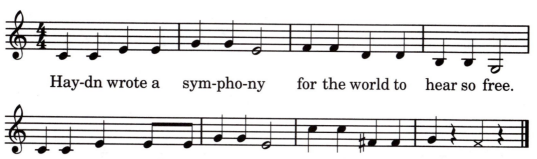

Hay-dn wrote a sym-pho-ny for the world to hear so free.

So the prince would-n't fall a-sleep, he made a sur-prise. Yeah!

Count & Play
Rhythm Activity Page

Tap Along

𝄞 Z Z Z Z | Z Z Z ___ | Z Z Z Z | Z Z Z ___

𝄞 Z Z Z Z | Z Z Z ___ | Z Z Z Z | Z ___ WOW

Say and Play

Fire Bird
(STRAVINSKY)

Lesson Plan

Objective: Students will recognize and perform long and short rhythms
($\quarternote$, $\halfnote$).

Materials: Piano
Copies of the *Fire Bird* Activity Page
Rhythm instruments

Procedure: 1. ***Tell the story*** of Fire Bird to the students.

2. ***Play the tune,*** and have the students tap along with the beat while you play the tune. Then ***teach the tune*** to the students.

3. ***Activity:*** Have the students tap the beat as they sing the tune. Ask them if the rhythm was even or uneven throughout the tune, and then have them tap the rhythm. Try having them tap the halfnotes and clap the quarternotes.

4. ***Activity:*** While using rhythm instruments such as bells or shakers, have the students play to the rhythm of the tune. Be sure they shake the instruments for a full two beats on the half notes.

5. ***Activity:*** Place the students in a circle or at their assigned spots with plenty of room. While singing the tune, have the student step for the short notes and stop for the long ones.

Activity Page: Use clapping and tapping or rhythm instruments with this activity.

Story of *Fire Bird*

Prince Ivan appears in the king's garden pursuing the Fire Bird. The Fire Bird dances while plucking golden apples from a magic tree in the garden. Suddenly, the dance breaks off when the prince catches her. They struggle, and the Fire Bird gives in to the prince.

The Fire Bird offers a feather to the prince as a pledge that she will help him if he were ever to need it. He accepts it, and she flies off.

Soon, thirteen captive princesses of the king appear in the garden playing a game with the golden apples. The prince appears, and the princesses dance with him. However, the prince becomes enchanted with the leader of the princesses—the one who is to be his bride.

In a panic, the princesses scurry back to the king's castle so as not to arouse his anger for their being late.

The prince decides to rescue his bride and free the captive princesses. So Ivan goes to the castle, opens the gates and attempts to start the rescue. The king is so infuriated that he begins to cast a spell which would turn Ivan to stone. But Ivan remembers his magic feather from the Fire Bird. No sooner does he wave it above his head than the king's spell is rendered powerless by the appearance and the magic of the Fire Bird.

Ivan and the princess marry. The Fire Bird leaves with a feeling of hope and joy.

Musical Excerpt from *Fire Bird*
IGOR STRAVINSKY (1882–1971)

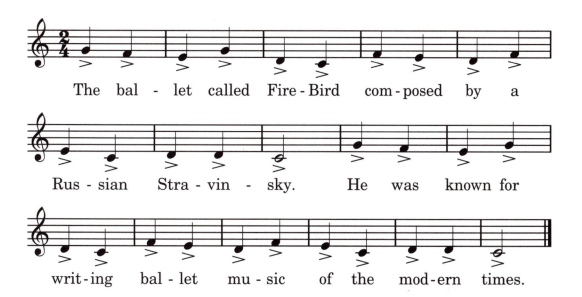

The bal - let called Fire - Bird com - posed by a

Rus - sian Stra - vin - sky. He was known for

writ - ing bal - let mu - sic of the mod - ern times.

Tap & Clap Activity Page

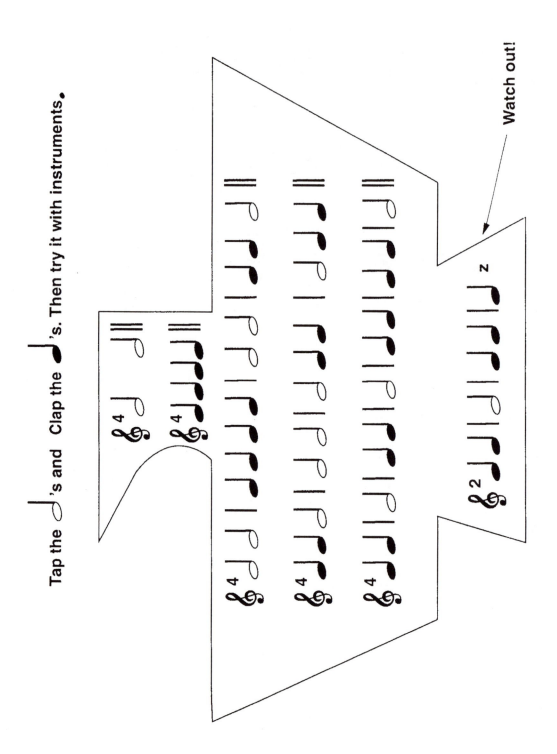

Don Giovanni
(MOZART)

Lesson Plan

Objective: Students will recognize and perform the tempo of slow.

Materials: Piano
Copies of the *Don Giovanni* Dot-to-Dot Activity Page
Pencils
Crayons

Procedure: 1. ***Tell the story*** of *Don Giovanni* to the students.

2. ***Play the tune.*** Ask the students: "Does the tune of *Don Giovanni* sound fast or slow?" Have the students use hand signals to indicate slow or fast (e.g., quick-chopping of the hands for fast and a crawling motion for slow).

3. ***Teach the tune.***

4. ***Activity:*** Have the students walk in place while singing the tune or other favorite songs which are slow.

5. ***Activity:*** Allow the students to move in a circle while you play familiar tunes or other songs with a variety of tempi—slow or fast. However, students should walk for slow music and stop for fast.

Activity Page: The students will connect the dots to both pictures. Have them decide which represents something that moves slow and which is a picture of the ghost of Don Giovanni.

Story of *Don Giovanni*

The story of *Don Giovanni* takes place in a small Spanish town. Don Giovanni was a bad, evil man who did many bad, evil things to people in his town. As he did more and more wrong things, people became more and more suspicious of him.

One day, Don Giovanni was invited to a masquerade dinner. All of the guests were disguised, and at first they could not identify one person from another. As the dinner went on, however, the guests began to discover who each person was. Also, people knew who Don Giovanni was and remembered what he had done in the past.

For years people had asked Don Giovanni to repent (to be sorry for what he had done), but he refused. However, during the dinner, without Don Giovanni's knowledge, a special guest was invited to the dinner. This guest was the ghost of a man whom Don Giovanni had wronged terribly when he was alive. This ghostly guest asked Don Giovanni to repent; afraid, he refused. Then the ghostly guest asked Don Giovanni to take his hand, and so he did. Don Giovanni felt the strong ice-cold clasp of the ghost's hand. Suddenly, smoke and fire flew; and Don Giovanni was gone.

Musical Excerpt from *Don Giovanni*
"Reich mir die Hand"
WOLFGANG AMADEUS MOZART
(1756–1791)

Moz-art he wrote an o - pera called Don Gi-o-van -

ni. The ghost shook the hand of Gi - o -

van - ni, and this aw-ful man was gone in a blink.

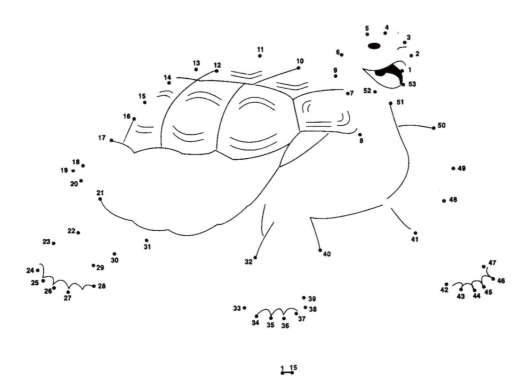

Don Giovanni
Dot-to-Dot Activity Page

Classic Tunes Level I Check-Up

After reviewing the first five classic tunes and tales over and over, it is time to find out how much the students have learned. Reproduce enough copies of the Tune Cards on the following page for each student. Cut out the cards and give each student a set.

NOTE: Tune cards for the next five classic tunes and tales in Level I are provided on page 27. These can be used for another check-up when you have completed the second half of this level

Use the cards to check students' recall as follows:

Explain to the students which tune each card represents.

Directions:

1. Play each tune one at a time.
2. Have the students raise the card that corresponds with the tune you play.
3. Be sure to count off or give a signal so students don't have time to look around at the others' answers.
4. Evaluate student response.
5. Periodically review the tunes.

Suggestion:

Reproduce the tune cards on oaktag and laminate—they will last longer. However, avoid color coding cards, in order to eliminate students' putting up the correct colors instead of the correct tune picture.

Tune Cards

William Tell Overture

**Eine Kleine
Nacht Music**

**Surprise
Symphony**

Fire Bird

Don Giovanni

Tune Cards

Minuet

1²³

Ode to Joy

Adagio

Swan Lake

Morning
Peer Gynt

Ode to Joy
(BEETHOVEN)

Lesson Plan

Objective: The students will perform and identify musical phrases.

Materials: Piano
                    Copies of the Musical Phrases Activity Page
                    Copies of the Beethoven Activity Page
                    Pencils
                    Crayons

Procedure: 1. **Tell the story** of *Ode to Joy* to the students.

                    2. **Teach the tune** to the students.

                    3. **Listen and sing** the tune as a class. Have the students walk to
                       the beat of the music until the end of each phrase—then stop.
                       Continue to walk and stop for each phrase.

                    4. **Define** a phrase. Explain that a musical phrase is a musical
                       sentence.

                    5. *Activity:* Have the students sing or listen to the tune while tap-
                       ping to the beat of the first phrase and clapping to the second.

                    6. *Activity:* While singing or listening to the tune, have the stu-
                       dents raise both hands and move left to right with the first
                       phrase (ends after the word "Germany"). Then have them move
                       their hands back, right to left, to end the second phrase ("...you
                       see").

Activity Page: Have the students draw curved lines for arches to indicate the the
                    beginning and end of each phrase of the tune.

Answer Key: Musical Phrases Activity Page Phrases end after "Germany" and
                    "see" (*Ode to Joy*); "sing" and "surprise" (*"Surprise" Symphony*).

Story of *Ode to Joy* (Symphony No. 9)

Beethoven was believed to be a very mean, strange, and crazy man during his lifetime. He avoided becoming friends, or even speaking to other people. Most people took his behavior to mean that he was weird, crazy, and a musical genius who was constantly thinking about music. But, there was a another reason for the way he acted.

It was said that Beethoven was writing a song for a singer, who was known for being a difficult person to deal with, and the singer became quite demanding, and required the composer to change the music many times. Eventually, Beethoven finally pleased the singer enough that he left, but suddenly a familiar knock came upon Beethoven's door. Beethoven knew the knock as the singer's knock, and he became so enraged that he threw himself on the floor. Many believed that he injured his ear when he fell to the floor so that he started to become deaf.

As Beethoven reached his twenties, he was becoming quite deaf. By the time he composed Symphony No. 9, he was completely deaf. So it would not be surprising to note that at the premiere (first performance) of the 9th Symphony, after the orchestra had finished the performance, the audience raved, applauded, and stood in excitement. Beethoven didn't realize the ovation he was receiving until his concertmaster (the first violinist in the orchestra) stood up and turned him toward his audience for a bow. Beethoven was so deaf he could not hear the applause of his audience. But he still knew his composition so well that his deafness could not diminish his ability to hear the music in his head.

Musical Excerpt from *Ode to Joy*
Symphony No. 9
Finale
LUDWIG VAN BEETHOVEN (1770–1827)

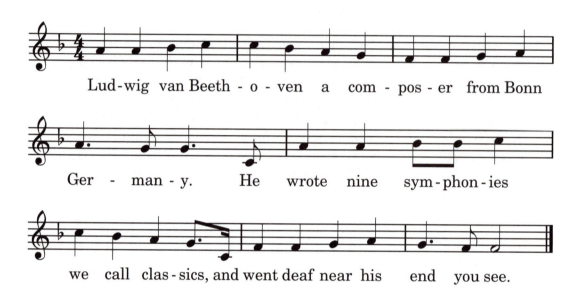

Lud-wig van Beeth - o - ven a com - pos - er from Bonn

Ger - man - y. He wrote nine sym - phon - ies

we call clas - sics, and went deaf near his end you see.

Musical Phrases Activity Page

𝄞 **Ludwig Van Beethoven a composer from Bonn Germany.**

𝄞 **He wrote nine symphonies we call music**
   went deaf near his end you see.

Haydn's Surprise Symphony

𝄞 **Haydn wrote a symphony**

𝄞 **For the world to hear and sing**

𝄞 **So the prince wouldn't fall asleep**

𝄞 **He made a surprise.**

Name _____

Beethoven Activity Page

Color this picture of Beethoven

Adagio
(BRAHMS)

Lesson Plan

Objective: The students will recognize and perform the term and tempo "adagio."

Materials: Piano
Rhythm instruments
Adagio Listening Examples
Copies of Adagio Tempo Activity Page

Procedure:
1. ***Tell the story*** to the students.
2. ***Teach the tune*** to the students.
3. ***Play the tune***. Ask the students whether it is fast or slow.
4. ***Activity:*** Using instruments (drums or rhythm sticks), echo a variety of rhythm patterns in adagio tempo.
5. ***Activity:*** Play a few songs the students know, and ask them if any could be adagio. Use the examples provided, or use some of your own. Have them respond by: standing for adagio and sitting for other.

Activity Page: Have the students fill in the blanks with the words that represent something that is slow. They may color in each letter of adagio as they come up with each word.

Answer Key: Adagio Tempo Activity Page
Molasses, Float (Creep or Crawl)
Turtle, Creep (Float or Crawl),
Crawl (Float or Creep), Slow.

Story of *Adagio*

Brahms wrote his First Symphony in 1876. Many people felt he had continued where Beethoven left off. It was believed so much that Brahm's First Symphony was nicknamed the Tenth (in reference to Beethoven's last symphony, the Ninth). It was in a letter Brahms wrote to Clara Schumann in 1868 that he included a gift of some music notation containing the theme of his First Symphony composed sometime later.

As a person, Brahms was known to be just the opposite of Beethoven. He was considered to be a kind, nice, generous, and thoughtful man. He was especially kind to children. Often, while taking his walks throughout the countryside, Brahms would be followed by a crowd of frolicking and eager young children. With his pockets full of treats and goodies, Brahms would toss about the rewards to the excited children. You can be sure he looked forward to those walks as much as his little friends.

The name of this tune is *Adagio*. It means "slowly."

Musical Excerpt from *Adagio*
Symphony No. 1
JOHANNES BRAHMS (1833–1897)

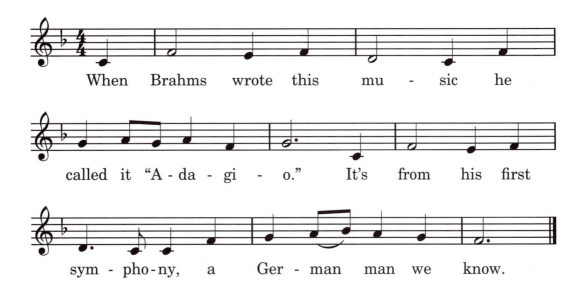

When Brahms wrote this mu - sic he called it "A - da - gi - o." It's from his first sym - pho-ny, a Ger - man man we know.

Adagio Listening Examples

© 1997 by Parker Publishing Company

Name _____

Adagio Tempo Activity Page

Fill in each group of blanks with the word that means slow or is slow. Color in the big letter for each word you come up with.

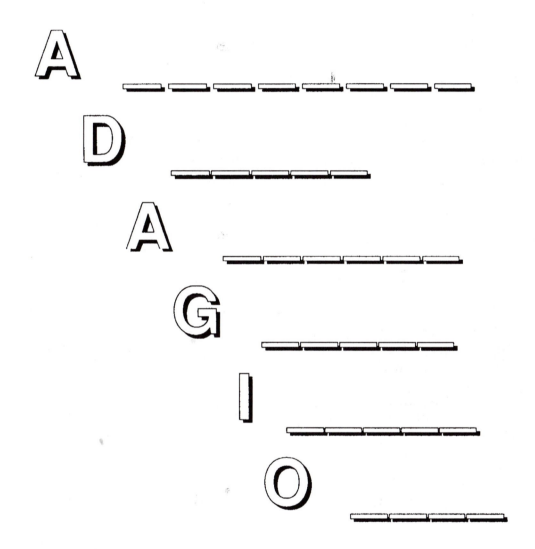

Adagio words

Molasses   Float   Turtle   Slow   Crawl   Creep

Swan Lake
(TCHAIKOVSKY)

Lesson Plan

Objective: Students will recognize the difference between Major(bright/happy) and Minor (dark/sad).

Materials: Piano
Copies of the Major/Minor Listening Activity Page
Pencils

Procedure: 1. *Tell the story* to the students.

2. *Teach the tune* to the students.

3. *Activity:* Play a variety of Major chords on the piano. Discuss the differences: bright, happy, and cheerful or dark, sad, and gloomy. Have the students respond by frowning for sad (Minor) and smiling for happy (Major).

4. *Sing* "Twinkle, Twinkle Little Star" and "Yankee Doodle" in Major and minor. Allow the students to differentiate the modes (Major/Minor).

Activity Page: Play five tunes on the piano. Have each student circle the sun for a bright/happy song or the clouds for a dark/sad song. Some suggestions of tunes to use: *Eine Kleine Nacht Musik, Swan Lake,* "*Bingo,*" and "*She'll Be Comin' Around the Mountain.*"

Story of *Swan Lake*

The story of *Swan Lake* takes place in Germany at about the time of Christopher Columbus. An old princess is concerned about her carefree son's avoidance or indifference to finding a wife and taking over the responsibilities for ruling the kingdom. The princess wants her son to choose a "wife to be" at the "coming of age ball" she is planning to hold.

During the ball the princess expects her son to be looking for a wife. She invites all the fairest young ladies in the kingdom. However, Siegfred, the prince, is not at all happy with the situation, so he decides to take a walk and do a little hunting. While walking, he becomes distracted by a flight of swans. He grabs his crossbow, and he pursues his game. Siegfred discovers that the swans are actually beautiful maidens, but, due to a spell, only assume human form at night. Without much delay, Siegfred falls in love with the queen of the swans, Odette, and convinces her that his love will release her from her spell's bond; she agrees. Odette also agrees to allow Siefred to accompany her to the ball so he can announce their engagement to be married. But an evil magician prevents her from attending the ball by disguising his daughter as Odette. The magician's daughter reveals who she is, and Siegfred becomes so shocked that he goes back to Odette at the lake. Odette tells Siegfried that the only way they can break the evil spell is to run off to a place where there are no other people. So the prince gives up his kingdom, and the couple runs away.

Musical Excerpt from *Swan Lake*
PETER ILLYICH TCHAIKOVSKY
(1840–1893)

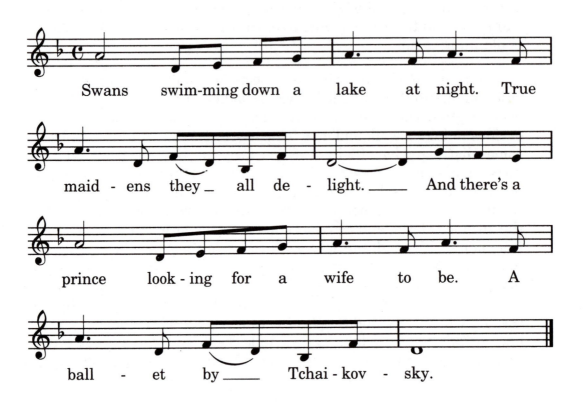

Swans swim-ming down a lake at night. True maid - ens they _ all de - light. _____ And there's a prince look - ing for a wife to be. A ball - et by _____ Tchai - kov - sky.

Swan Lake Bright/Dark Examples

Twinkle Twinkle Little Star

Yankee Doodle

Major/Minor Listening Activity Page

Circle the sun for a bright, happy song.
Circle the clouds for a dark, gloomy song.

1.

2.

3.

4.

5.

Peer Gynt
(GRIEG)

Lesson Plan

Objective: Students will distinguish low and high melodic direction.

Materials: Piano
Tone bells
Copies of High and Low Listening Activity Page
Pencils

Procedure:

1. ***Tell the story*** of *Peer Gynt* to the students.

2. ***Teach the tune*** to the students.

3. ***Focus the lesson*** on low and high pitches and melodic direction. Demonstrate low to high and high to low melodic lines. Use tone bells C, D, E, and G.

4. ***Activity:*** Play a few ascending and descending sequences on the piano. Have the students raise their hands to ascending (rising) sequences and lower their hands for descending ones. Also, try having them stand or sit for ascending or descending sequences. You may want to try excerpts from *Peer Gynt's* "Morning" or other tunes that are appropriate.

5. ***Game:*** Select one student to cover his or her eyes with a blindfold. Pick another student to play the bells either in an ascending order or a descending order. The blindfolded student guesses whether the bells sounded in an upward motion or a downward motion. Have all the other students show the correct answer by using thumbs up for ascending and thumbs down for descending. Allow the student to select the next player for the game.

Activity Page: The purpose of this activity page is to help students hear and see low to high and high to low. For the top section, play five melodic lines that ascend or descend. Have the students circle the steps that go in the direction of the melody.

On part two of the activity page, have the students draw a line going up or down in the direction of the notated melodies.

6. ***Examples of melodic lines:***

Answer Key: High and Low Listening Activity Page

1. Low to High	2. High to Low	3. Low to High
4. Low to High	5. High to Low	6. Low to High
7. High to Low	8. Low to High	9. Low to High
10. High to Low		

Story of *Peer Gynt* (Suite No. 1) "Morning"

Peer Gynt was a boastful Norweigian folk hero who was a chronic liar. Peer lived with his elderly mother Aase. On the day of the wedding of his former girlfriend, Ingrid, he kidnaps her and takes her off to the mountains. After she escapes, he becomes an outlaw and gets involved in various adventures.

One such adventure includes an episode with the troll king's daughter in the Hall of the Mountain King. The trolls (Scandinavian mythical beings) attack him, but the ringing church bells frighten the trolls away.

Peer then goes to the woods to live, and there he is followed by the faithful Solveig, who is in love with him. Soon he deserts her and returns home. Upon returning home he discovers his mother is gravely ill; and shortly after, she dies.

Following his mother's death, Peer runs off to America, Africa, and other places. When he finally returns home for the last time, he is an old feeble man who realizes he has wasted his life, but his devoted and faithful Solveig is still there to redeem him and his life.

© 1997 by Parker Publishing Company

Musical Excerpt from *Peer Gynt* Suite No. 1 "Morning"
EDVARD GRIEG (1843–1907)

Grieg wrote a qui - et tune; from his Peer Gynt Suite

from Nor-way's myth-o - lo - gy. It is called morn-ing so

qui - et and sun - ny, just start-ing a new _____ day.

High and Low Listening Activity Page

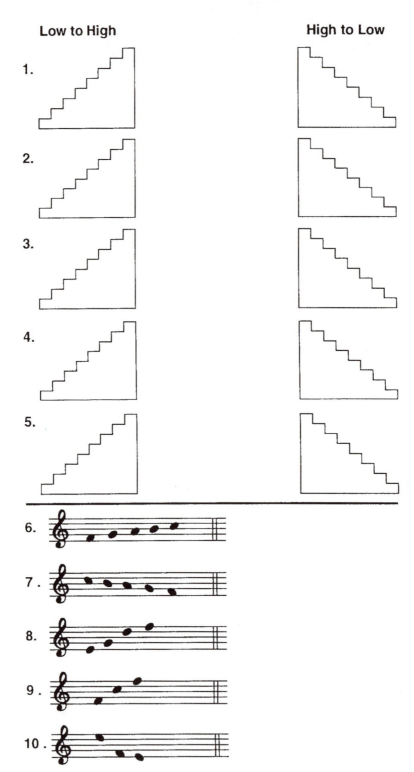

Low to High

High to Low

1.

2.

3.

4.

5.

6.

7.

8.

9.

10.

Little Minuet
(BACH)

Lesson Plan

Objective: Students will read and perform meter in 3 (strong-weak-weak).

Materials: Piano
Copies of Meter in 3 Activity Page
Drums and/or rhythm sticks

Procedure:
1. ***Tell the story*** to the students.
2. ***Teach the tune*** to the students.
3. ***Focus the lesson*** on triple meter/strong-weak-weak.
4. ***Activity:*** Do the following rhythm pattern: Clap on beat one, snap on beats two and three. Encourage the students to join you until everyone is performing the rhythm. Ask probing questions to assist students in discovering the meter of 3 and the placement of the strong and weak beats. "What is the snap and clap pattern?" "Which is the strongest?" "If we count 1,2,3 for the beats, which is the strongest?"
5. ***Activity:*** Have the students tap their legs and clap their hands in three. Ask the students to hop, clap, clap in three. Pair up the students. Have them clap their own hands on one, and clap their left then right hands on two and three, respectfully, with their partners.

Activity Page: Use drums or rhythm sticks, and have the students drum or snap on one, two, and three.

Story of *Little Minuet*

Johann Sebastian Bach was a German composer born in a family with a deep heritage in religion, academics, and music, in that order. Music was the guide or tool they used to celebrate and devote themselves to their religion. Bach wrote for numerous genre (types of instruments and groups) including: keyboard instruments, orchestra, and the voice. Although he wrote a great deal of secular (non-religious) music, his composition was imbedded in his passion for sacred music (religious music).

The Little Minuet is one of Bach's finest and most popular secular pieces performed by pianists, orchestras, and other musicians throughout the world today. The minuet was a dance that Bach included in his suites (groups of pieces) for which he composed or transcribed for many instruments. The roots of the minuet originated in the seventeenth century French court.

Bach, although a very kind person, had a hot, quick temper. Once in a while he would become involved in spats and altercations. One such spat took place with an organist he was working with. The organist was a good player, but one particular time he played a terrible sounding chord that enraged Bach so that he tore off the wig on his head and threw it at the organist and said: "You should be making shoes, not music."

Musical Excerpt from *Little Minuet*
JOHANN SEBASTIAN BACH
(1685–1750)

Meter in 3 Activity Page

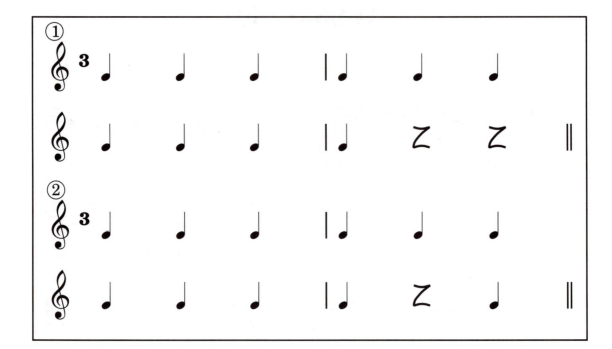

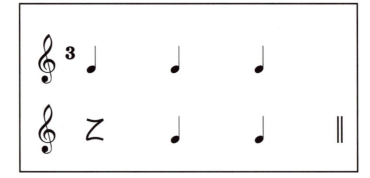

Classic Tunes Level I Test

Directions: Give each student a copy of the Level I Tunes Test Activity Page on page 52, then proceed as follows:

1. Review what each picture represents with the students.

2. Play the ten tunes of Level I in any order; however, be sure to notate what the tune order is, in order to recall each for correcting papers.

3. Have the students write the corresponding number under the picture that represents the tune heard in its order.

   NOTE: It is a good practice to constantly review the tunes as you add more to a class's repertoire.

4. Following the test, play each tune again. Allow the students to name the composer orally for each tune.

Level I Tunes Test Activity Page

Surprise Symphony

Adagio

Fire Bird

Minuet

William Tell Overture

Don Giovanni

Ode to Joy

Swan Lake

Peer Gynt

Eine Kleine Nacht Music

LEVEL II:
(GRADE LEVELS: 2-3)

The Trout
(SCHUBERT)

Lesson Plan

Objective: Students will identify steps and skips in music.

Materials: Piano
An octave of tone bells
Copies of the Stairstep Model and Skip/Step Examples
A staff
Copies of the Steps and Skips Activity Page
Pencils

Procedure:
1. ***Tell the story*** of *The Trout* to the students.
2. ***Teach the tune*** to the students.
3. *Activity:* Use the stairsteps and notes to help the students recognize steps and skips. Do a variety of examples of steps and skips for the students, and then have them try a few. Photocopy the stairstep model for each student or have students go to the board on an individual basis. Examples are given on the following pages.
4. *Activity:* Use a music staff to assist in transferring the step and skip theory to music. As a class or individually, place 2, 3, 4, or 5 notes on a staff in step or skip patterns.
5. *Activity:* Demonstrate a series of steps and skips on an octave of bells. Allow students the opportunity to visually witness what steps and skips are on the bells. Then permit students to guess which examples you play. Finally, give students a chance to play a step or skip pattern on the bells, and allow the rest of the class to respond by putting their hands together for steps and apart for skips.

Activity Page: Have the students circle the skips and put the squares around the steps.

Answer Key: Steps and Skips Activity Page (left to right/top to bottom) step, skip, skip, skip, step, skip, step, skip, skip, step

Story of *The Trout*

Back in the early 1800's Franz Schubert took a happy journey through upper Austria enjoying the landscape of the country. His infatuation with nature may have led to the writing of his art song called *The Trout*. During his trip through Austria, he was asked to write the tune of *The Trout* for string quartet and piano (a quintet, music for five performers). It has become one of the grandest and most popular pieces of chamber music.

Schubert was living in the city of Vienna, Austria, when Beethoven died. As a matter of fact, he attended the funeral of the great composer. Following the funeral, he and a few friends, who also attended went to an inn for dinner. Schubert raised his glass and proposed a toast to "the one whom we buried today." He proposed a second toast to "the one who will go next." Less than two years later, Schubert was dead at the age of thirty-one.

Musical Excerpt from *The Trout*
FRANZ SCHUBERT (1797–1828)

Stairstep Model

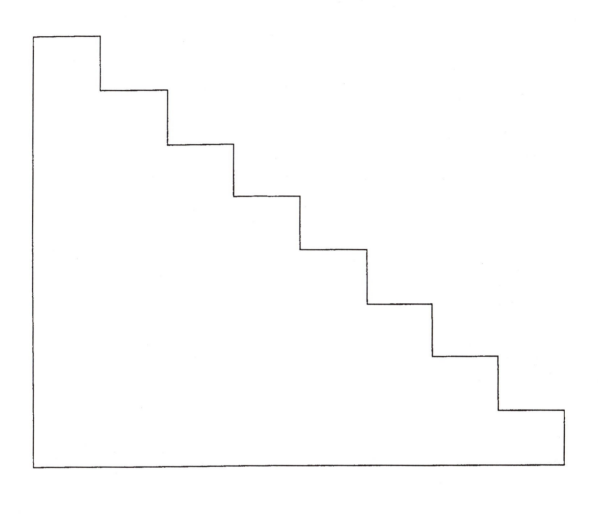

Skip Example

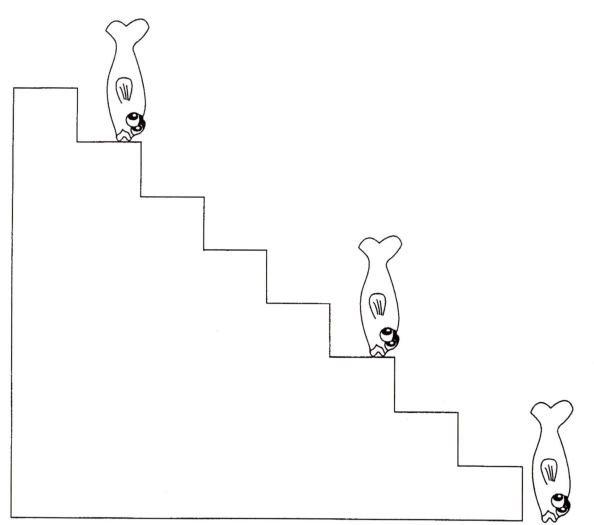

Step Example

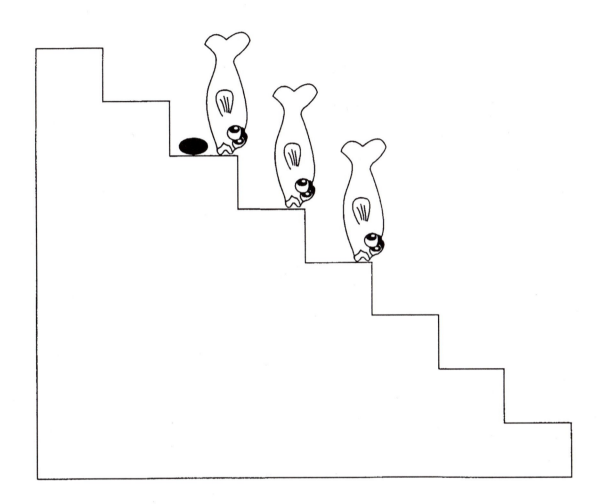

Skip Example

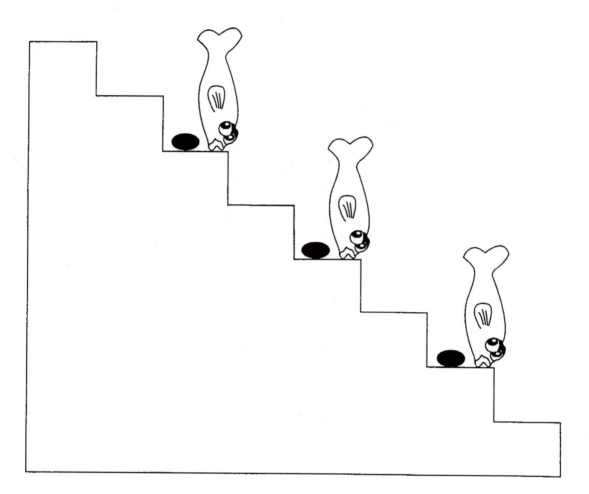

Step and Skip Example

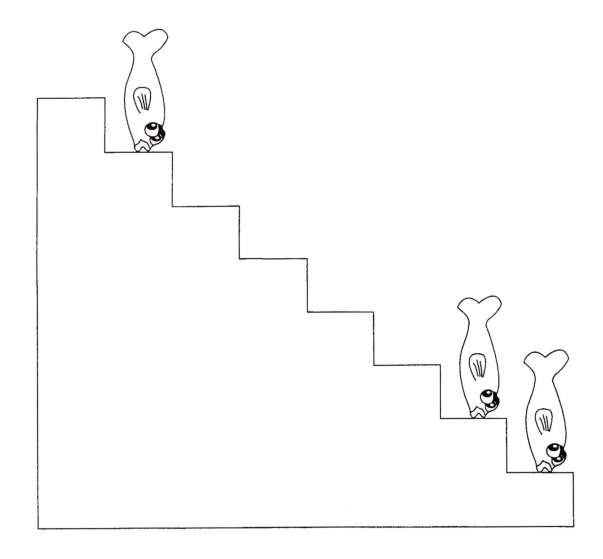

Name _____

Steps and Skips Activity Page

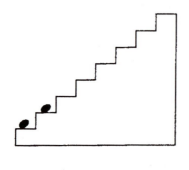
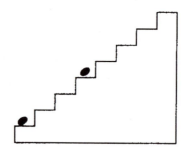

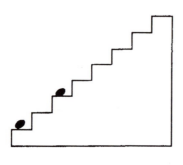
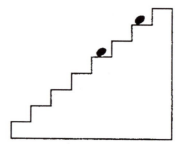

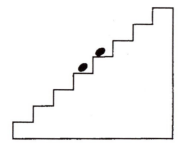
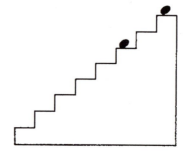

Trumpet Voluntary
(CLARKE)

Lesson Plan

Objective: Students will identify the trumpet as a brass instrument.

Materials: Piano
Copies of the Trumpet/Brass Family Activity Page
Copies of the Trumpet Coloring Page
Two different lengths of rubber hose
Pictures of brass instruments
Trumpet
Crayons

Procedure:

1. ***Tell the story*** of *Trumpet Vountary* to the students.

2. ***Teach the tune*** phrase by phrase; words then music.

3. ***Focus the lesson*** on the trumpet. Use the trumpet to explain why it is a brass instrument. Demonstrate how to buzz the lips in order to produce a sound on the trumpet.

4. ***Activity:*** Give each student a copy of the trumpet page. Lead the class through a voyage of the trumpet's air flow by drawing a line from the mouthpiece to the bell, while passing through the leadpipe and valves.

5. ***Activity:*** Take a thin, narrow piece of hose, and place the mouthpiece of a brass instrument in one end and buzz and blow through it. Twist and turn the tube to demonstrate the sound. Also, show the difference between a longer hose and a shorter one. Relate this information to a brass instrument. Discuss the similarities of the trumpet with other brass instruments (use pictures of the other brass instruments).

Activity Page: Have the students color the trumpet yellow. Also, instruct them to color the other instruments that are members of the brass family yellow.

Story of *Trumpet Voluntary*

Jeremiah Clarke's *Trumpet Voluntary* remains a popular wedding processional and recessional today. Originally, his *Voluntary* was thought to be composed by the more famous English composer Henry Purcell.

The voluntary is an old English organ piece that was composed or improvised before, during, or after church services during the sixteenth to the nineteenth centuries. The word "voluntary" refers to natural growth or spontaneous growth.

Clarke's *Trumpet Voluntary* contains a clarino part. This part was typically composed of the upper, or the higher, notes played on the Baroque trumpet. It was also used during the Middle Ages and the Renaissance—twelfth to eighteenth centuries.

Musical Excerpt
from *Trumpet Voluntary*
JEREMIAH CLARKE (1673–1707)

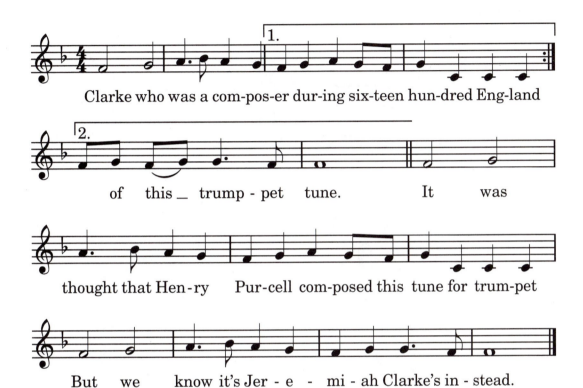

Clarke who was a com-pos-er dur-ing six-teen hun-dred Eng-land

of this _ trump - pet tune. It was

thought that Hen-ry Pur-cell com-posed this tune for trum-pet

But we know it's Jer - e - mi - ah Clarke's in - stead.

Name _____

Trumpet/Brass Family Activity Page

Color the picture of the trumpet yellow. Also color yellow any other instruments you see that are members of the brass family.

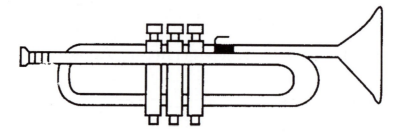

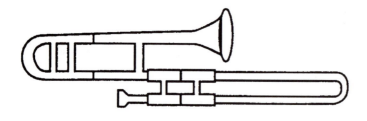

Trumpet Coloring Page

Color this picture of the trumpet.

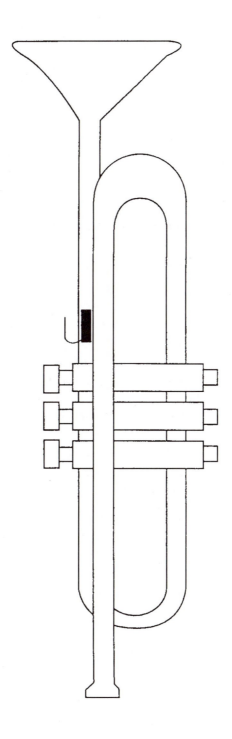

Happy Farmer
(SCHUMANN)

Lesson Plan

Objective: Students will recognize and perform first and second endings:

Materials: Piano
Chalkboard
Music text
Copies of the First and Second Endings Activity Page

Procedure: 1. ***Tell the story*** of *Happy Farmer* to the students.

2. ***Teach the tune*** to the students.

3. ***Activity:*** Have the students clap and tap the following rhythm. Then have them repeat it; however, end it differently.

4. ***Activity:*** Write both the first and second clap, tap, and snap examples given in the previous activity on the board. Point out the similar measures and the different ones. Erase the second line and show the students how this music notation shorthand is written by adding the brackets; thus, saving space and work for the musician.

5. ***Activity:*** Using a basic music textbook, conduct a search for songs that utilize the first and second endings notation.

6. ***Activity Page:*** Instruct the students to tap along on the notes while you clap or play the rhythm on the piano for exercises 1 and 2. Exercise 3's first and second endings are to be completed by the student.

Story of *Happy Farmer*

Robert Schumann was a piano student so eager to become one of the finest musicians of his time that he invented a contraption or little device that would hold his fourth finger (ring finger) immobile while his other fingers continued to play. The pupose of the device was to make the finger more independent and stronger, since the fourth finger is the least independent and weakest of the fingers for playing the piano. However, the gadget was so effective that it injured Schumann's finger permanently, thus ending his hopes to become a famous performer.

Schumann then turned to composing and began a well-repected and intense career. He became a nervous and moody man who had to relinquish music posts due to the fact that he could not work in public. As he became older, Schumann began to hallucinate sounds. He would quite often wake up in the middle of the night hearing or imagining sounds, and he would immediately go to write them down.

At one point, Schumann was so maddened and depressed that he tried to commit suicide by throwing himself into the Rhine River. Fortunately, a local fisherman rescued him and placed him in a private hospital. Two years later, he died after establishing himself as one of the great Romantic period composers.

Musical Excerpt from *Happy Farmer*
ROBERT SCHUMANN (1810–1856)

When Schu - mann wrote the Hap-py Farm-er song, he

wrote it for the key-board and it's not too long.   not too long.

Name _____

First and Second Endings
Activity Page

Directions: Tap along with the teacher on numbers 1 and 2. Be sure to repeat and watch your endings.

Fill in the first and second endings with two beats each. Remember— be sure they are different. Choose measures from the note bank.

Note Bank

Fifth Symphony
(BEETHOVEN)

Lesson Plan

Objective: Students will identify the instrument families of the symphony orchestra.

Materials: Piano
Copies of the Instrument Families Activity Page
A string instrument (if possible)
A brass instrument
A woodwind instrument
A percussion instrument
Copies of the Instrument Card Pages
Pencils

Procedure: 1. **Tell the story** of the *Fifth Symphony* to the students.

2. **Teach the tune** to the students.

3. **Focus the lesson** on and discuss the symphony orchestra's instrumental families. With the use of instruments or pictures of instruments, discuss the characteristics of each family. This can be done as a class or in groups assigned to do a particular family.

4. **Activity:** Take two instrument photos from an orchestra family and two from another. Create as many of these two vs. two instrument families as needed. Assign students to different stations where two vs. two photos are located. Mix the photos up. Allow the students to group the photos into two families, and name the family by looking at the characteristics of the instruments. Combine the groups again into a class, and discuss the characteristics and names of the families and why the names were selected.

5. **Activity:** Use the Instrument Card Pages to photocopy enough cards so each student has one. Sing a sentence, for example, "Who has a brass instrument?" on whatever melody, pitches, or intervals appropriate to your program. Have those students respond by raising their cards. Also, have the students sing "I have a brass instrument." Continue this with all the families, and continue the activity again. You may eventually want to expand this activity to include individual instruments.

Activity Page:	Have the students write the corresponding characteristics with the correct instrument families.
Answer Key:	*Brass:* buzz lips to produce sound, made of brass, bell-shaped on the end, are pitched instruments, valves are pressed.
	Woodwinds: use a reed, holes are covered by the fingers, some are bell-shaped on the end, some are made of metal, wood or plastic, are pitched instruments, can use two reeds.
	Percussion: are struck together to produce a sound, are beaten with mallets or sticks, some are made of metal, wood or plastic, are pitched instruments, are non-pitched.
	Strings: a bow is used, use a bridge, are pitched, use strings.

Story of the *Fifth Symphony*

Beethoven was born in Bonn, Germany, where his father and grandfather were singers at the court of the Elector (political position). The family life was not a good one. His father was an alcoholic, and Ludwig was forced to work to help support the family. He got a job as an organist, and later became the harpsichordist for the Elector's orchestra. At age seventeen, Beethoven travelled to Vienna where he had an opportunity to play for Mozart. Mozart was so impressed that he said, "This boy will make a big noise in the world some day." Some years later it was arranged for Beethoven to study with Hadyn in Vienna, and he never returned home to Germany again.

Beethoven worked for many of the aristocratic music patrons by performing, teaching, and composing. However, his volcanic and turbulent temperament was quite evident. It's been said that when he was performing at the home of a count, a noble was constantly talking. Beethoven became so enraged, he stopped playing and remarked, "For such pigs I do not play."

His twilight years brought problems with publishers and total deafness, and this triggered a more frustrated and irritable man. A ride in an open carriage in bad weather brought on an illness that proved to be fatal. He died at age 57. Beethoven's *Fifth Symphony* is probably the most popular symphony in history. Its powerful first four notes make it uniquely recognizable and moving.

Musical Excerpt
from the *Fifth Symphony*
LUDWIG VAN BEETHOVEN
(1770–1827)

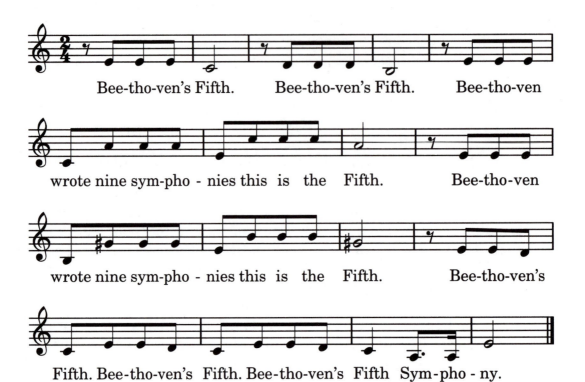

Bee-tho-ven's Fifth.   Bee-tho-ven's Fifth.   Bee-tho-ven

wrote nine sym-pho - nies this is   the   Fifth.   Bee-tho-ven

wrote nine sym-pho - nies this is   the   Fifth.   Bee-tho-ven's

Fifth. Bee-tho-ven's Fifth. Bee-tho-ven's Fifth Sym-pho - ny.

Instrument Families Activity Page

Directions: Write the instrument characteristics in the box that best fits the instrument family. Some answers may be used for more than one family.

Instrument Characteristics

buzz lips to produce the sound
use a reed
a bow is used
are struck together to produce a sound
are beaten with mallets or sticks
made of brass
use a bridge
holes are covered by the fingers

some are bell-shaped on the end
some are made of metal, wood or plastic
are pitched instruments
use strings
can use two reeds
valves are pressed
some are non-pitched instruments

Brass

Woodwinds

Percussion

Strings

Instrument Card Page

  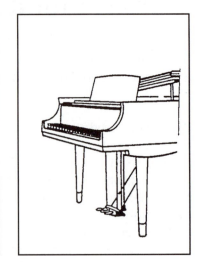

 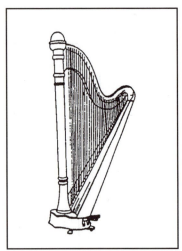 

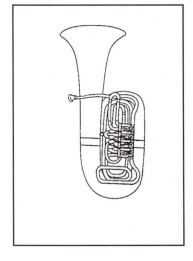  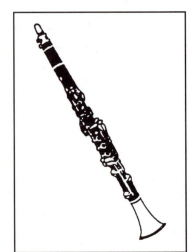

Instrument Card Page

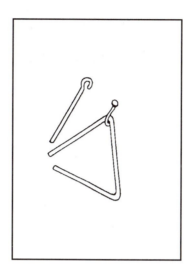

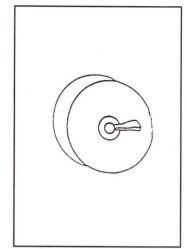

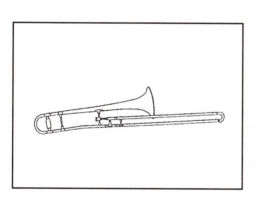

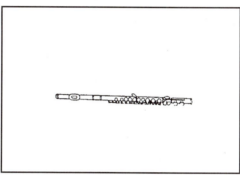

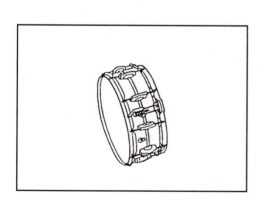

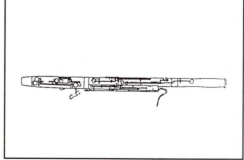

Symphony No. 2 (RACHMANINOFF)

Lesson Plan

Objective: Students will read and perform the dynamic markings of piano, forte, crescendo, and decrescendo.

Materials: Piano
Pencils
Copies of the Loud and Soft Activity Page
Copies of the Focus Page
Copies of the Forte/Piano Cards on the Dynamics Cards Page

Procedure: 1. *Tell the story* of the *Second Symphony* to the students.

2. *Teach the tune* to the students. Be sure the students sing the tune piano (soft) the first time and forte (loud) the second time through.

3. *Focus the lesson* on performing as well as reading piano and forte. Use the Focus Page to help students read and sing loudly and softly. Remind them that dynamics are like the volume button on the television set.

4. *Activity: Play various examples* (use previously learned tunes) of piano or forte. Allow the students to raise the card that corresponds with the appropriate dynamic level.

5. *Game:* Choose a student to hide his/her eyes. Pick another student to hold an object (possibly, a dynamic card). Have the student sing the tune over and over. Have the hiding student walk around the room to find the person with the object. As the walker gets closer, have the class sing louder; as the walker gets farther away from the object, the class sings quieter.

Activity Page: Have the students *circle* any pictures or symbols that can be considered loud and *box in* any item representing soft.

Story of *Symphony No. 2*

The composer Rachmaninoff was born in Russia in 1873. His father and grandfather were gifted pianists, so it's no surprise that Rachmaninoff became one of the great pianists and piano composers of his day. At the age of nine he studied at Moscow Conservatory where students wore uniforms, lived in one large room, and were supervised when they practiced.

In 1905, the Russian Revolution began to explode. By 1906, Rachmaninoff felt the pressure of the revolution, so he moved his family to Dresden, Germany. While there, he composed his Second Symphony and soon afterwards toured the world. He returned to Russia in 1910.

The Russian leader, or tsar, was deposed in the Revolution of 1917, and a tour was set up for Rachmaninoff which allowed him to escape Russia and go into exile. He and his family boarded a sleigh and crossed the border into Finland, never to return to their homeland again.

Rachmaninoff lived in Europe for a short time, then moved to the United States. Although he was comfortable and safe in the United States, he always had an ache in his heart caused by his longing for Russia. Pessimistic and broken, Rachmaninoff composed very little during his last 25 years. After a 1943 concert tour in the U.S., he returned home to Beverly Hills, California, where he died from cancer.

Musical Excerpt from *Symphony No. 2*
SERGEI RACHMANINOFF
(1873–1943)

Rach-ma-ni-noff did write this sec-ond sym,-pho-ny. _ A sla-vic

com-po-ser from Rus-sian land. Born in a fam-i-ly known for their

pi - a - nists. And he be - came   one _ of the great-est.

Focus Page

Dynamics Cards Page

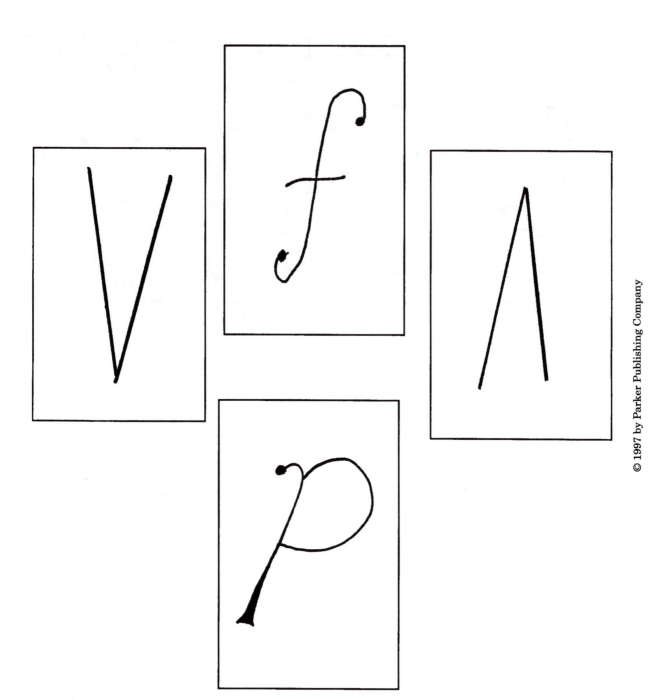

Name _____

Loud and Soft Activity Page

(Circle) all of the forte (loud) pictures and symbols.

[Box] in all of the piano (soft) pictures or symbols.

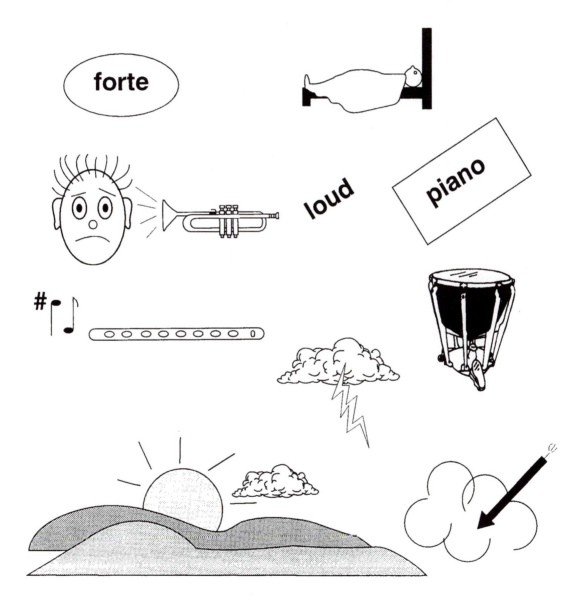

Classic Tunes Level II
LISTENING QUIZ
Teacher's Edition

Give each student a copy of the following Listening Quiz Activity Page.

Then play each of the tunes listed below for the students. They are to choose the correct title from the tune list and match it with the appropriate composer.

Use the copy of the quiz below to record the order in which you play each tune.

Title	*Composer*
1. *Happy Farmer*	Schumann
2. *Trumpet Voluntary*	Clarke
3. *The Trout*	Schubert
4. *Fifth Symphony*	Beethoven
5. *Symphony No. 2*	Rachmaninoff

Tunes

The Trout   *Symphony No. 2*
Fifth Symphony   *Trumpet Voluntary*
Happy Farmer

Classic Tunes Level II
Listening Quiz Activity Page

Title   *Composer*

1. _____   Schumann

2. _____   Clarke

3. _____   Schubert

4. _____   Beethoven

5. _____   Rachmaninoff

Titles Bank

Fifth Symphony   Symphony No. 2
The Trout   Trumpet Voluntary

Happy Farmer

Canon in D
(PACHELBEL)

Lesson Plan

Objective: Students will perform a circle canon through the use of the repeat sign ‖: :‖

Materials: Piano
Music to "Row, Row, Row Your Boat" and "Frere Jacques"
Music textbook
Copies of the *Canon in D* Activity Page

Procedure:
1. ***Tell the story*** of *Canon in D* to the students.
2. ***Teach the tune*** to the students phrase by phrase; first the words, then the music.
3. ***Activity:*** Explain what a round is and how it works, and sing an example of one, such as: "Row, Row, Row Your Boat" or "Frere Jacques." Eventually, use *Canon in D* to have the students practice it as a circle canon or a round.
4. ***Activity:*** Use your music textbook or some other source. Have the students search for songs they believe are rounds. Also, have them look for the repeat signs ‖: :‖

Activity Page: Teach the students what the symbol ‖: :‖ means and how to perform it. Have the students sing *Canon in D* using the activity page. Emphasize the repeats.

Story of *Canon in D*

Johann Pachelbel was a German organist and composer who lived during the Baroque Period. He was known to have been a great influence on Johann Sebastian Bach. His best known work is *Canon in D.*

A canon is a music composition which imitates a phrase or line in a different voice or voices. One type of canon popular today is the round. A round is a circle canon; it continuously returns to the beginning. "Row, Row, Row Your Boat" and "Frere Jacques" are two good examples of circle canons, or rounds.

Musical Excerpt from *Canon in D*
JOHANN PACHELBEL (1653–1716)

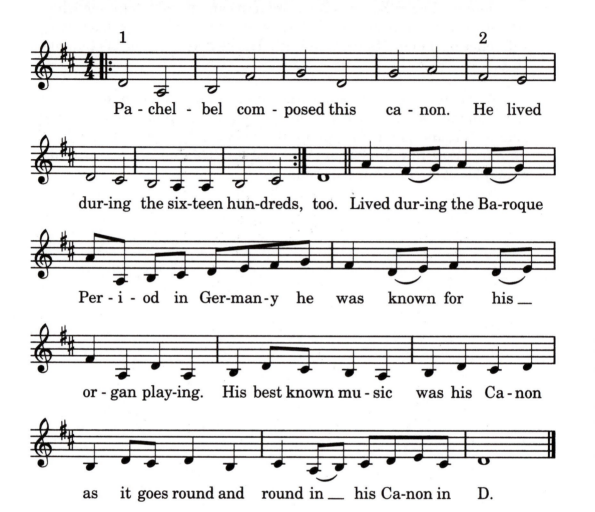

Pa - chel - bel com - posed this ca - non. He lived dur-ing the six-teen hun-dreds, too. Lived dur-ing the Ba-roque Per - i - od in Ger-man-y he was known for his — or - gan play-ing. His best known mu - sic was his Ca - non as it goes round and round in — his Ca-non in D.

Canon in D Activity Page

1. ‖: Pachelbel composed this canon. He lived during the sixteen hundreds :‖ , too.

2.

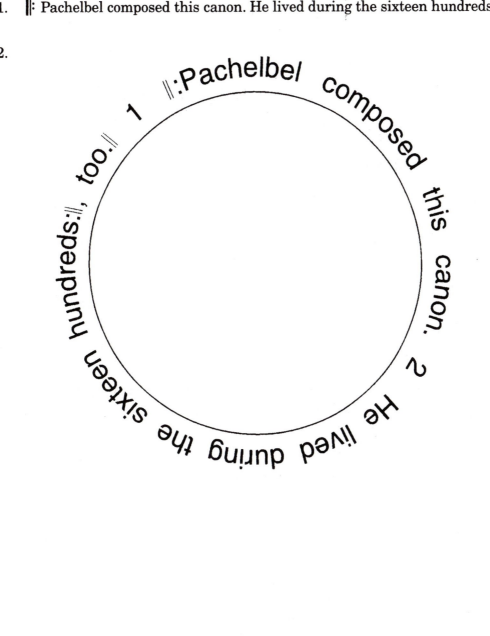

Rodeo
(COPLAND)

Lesson Plan

Objective: Students will perform the rhythms ♫♫, ♩♫, ♫ .

Materials: Piano
Copies of the Rhythm Cards
Copies of the *Rodeo* Activity Page

Procedure:
1. **Tell the story** of *Rodeo* to the students.
2. **Teach the tune** to the students.
3. **Note:** This particular lesson will take some preparation. You may find it more prudent to use it as a follow-up or supplementary lesson.
4. **Echo clap** the following rhythms with the students.

5. **Review** the counting syllables for the rhythms. ♫♫ (1e+a or ti-ka-ti-ka), ♩♫ (1 +a or ti ti-ka), and ♫♩ (1e+ or ti-ka ti). Use the rhythm cards to assist in your review.
6. **Game:** Using the Rhythm Cards, choose one student to start the game by picking a rhythm card from a stack of hidden ones. He/she must clap or say the rhythm. If it is correct, the class will give the thumbs up sign. If the student is incorrect, thumbs down. The student will then select the next person and sit in that person's seat.

Activity Page: Have the students clap or use a rhythm instrument to perform each line of music.

Story of *Rodeo*

Rodeo is a ballet for which the music was written by the American composer Aaron Copland. It was first produced in 1942.

The ballet is about about a cowgirl who is neglected and lonely, and who usually dresses in cowboy pants and a shirt. She is attending a Saturday night dance and is watching the couples dancing; but nobody wants to dance with her. Her friend, the Champion Roper, takes pity on her and shows her a few steps. Then she sees the Head Wrangler, who she is infatuated with, dancing with the Head Rancher's daughter. The cowgirl then runs away sobbing while everybody else continues to dance. When the cowgirl returns, the dancers all stop and look at her in surprise. They see her wearing a dress for the first time, and she also has a bow in her hair. Suddenly, everybody believes her to be a sort of Cinderella of the West. The Head Wrangler notices her beauty and becomes very interested; however, so does the Champion Roper. Both men try to win her fancy. In the end, she settles on the Roper—the only one who has ever shown her any attention.

Copland has been known for being America's foremost ballet composer of the twentieth century. In addition to composing the music to *Rodeo,* he wrote the music to the ballets *Billy the Kid* and *Appalachian Spring.*

Musical Excerpt
from *Rodeo* (Hoedown)
AARON COPLAND (1900–1990)

Cop - land an A - mer - i - can com - po - ser.

Ro - de - o was a bal - let he wrote.

Cow - boys danc - ing in a Hoe - down.

Wrote this mu - sic in Nine-teen For - ty Two.

Rhythm Cards

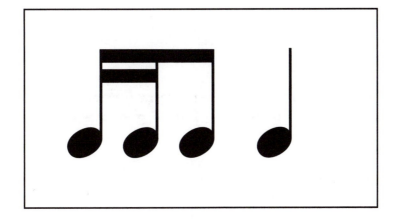

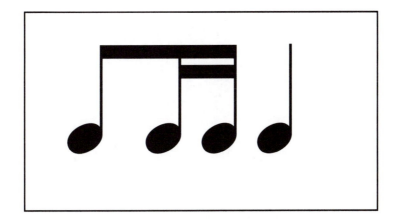

Rodeo Activity Page

The Nutcracker (TCHAIKOVSKY)

Lesson Plan

Objective: Students will recognize the music and identify the essential concepts of the ballets: *Rodeo, Fire Bird, Swan Lake*, and *Nutcracker*.

Materials: Piano
Copies of The Ballets Activity Page

Procedure: 1. ***Tell the story*** of the Nutcracker to the students.

2. ***Teach the tune*** to the students.

3. ***Explain*** to the students that ballet is a dance that tells a story and is accompanied by music.

4. ***Play*** excerpts from *Fire Bird, Swan Lake*, and *Rodeo* for the students. Ask them to identify each tune and composer.

5. ***Activity:*** Group students in four or eight teams. Assign each team a ballet. Have the students review the story and its characters. Bring the class together again, and discuss each ballet.

6. ***Follow-up activity:*** Using the teams formed earlier, have the groups take their assigned ballet and list what would be needed to produce the ballet. Also, you may want them to act out their ballet story.

Activity Page: Have the students put the words that best fit the appropriate ballet in the correct box.

Story of *The Nutcracker*

The Nutcracker is a ballet that takes place in a house where a Christmas party is occurring. Following the exchange of toys for the children, Uncle Drosslemeyer gives the girl, Clara, an old-fashioned nutcracker. Her brother, Fritz, squabbles with her and breaks the nutcracker. After the party is over and the guests have gone home, Clara returns back downstairs and nurses her broken nutcracker.

At the stroke of midnight, mice invade the entire room and turn into the size of humans. These creatures are led by the three-headed Mouse King into a battle against the Nutcracker and the other toys, but the Nutcracker and his friends win the fight because Clara throws her shoe and hits the Mouse King, destroying him and his leadership. The battle ends, and the Nutcracker turns back into a handsome prince and takes Clara through the Wintry Forest to the Kingdom of Sweets, ruled by the Sugar Plum Fairy. There they are entertained by Arabian, Chinese, Spanish, Russian, Flute, and Flower dances.

Musical Excerpt
from *The Nutcracker* ("March")
PETER I. TCHAIKOVSKY (1840–1893)

It's Tchai-kov-sky's Bal - let Nut - crack - er.

It's Tchai-kov-sky's Bal - let Nut - crack - er. The

March is when the mice come in at-tack-ing Clar-a and her friends. They

fight and fight, but Clar - a wins be - cause she threw her shoe.

The Ballets Activity Page

Put the words that best describe the ballets in the correct boxes.

Rodeo	Fire Bird	Swan Lake	Nutcracker

Cowgirl

Sugar Plum Fairy

Wrangler

Swan Princess

Magic Feather

Prince

Champion Roper

Christmas

Evil Spell

Golden Apples

Hoedown

Mouse King

Rancher

King's Garden

Captive Princesses

Fantasie-Impromptu
(CHOPIN)

Lesson Plan

Objective: Students will identify the note values: whole note, half note, and quarter note.

Materials: Piano
Copies of the tune
Copies of the Note Value Cards Page
Copies of the Music Pizzas Page
Copies of the Note Values Activity Page

Procedure:
1. ***Tell the story*** to the students.
2. ***Teach the tune*** to the students.
3. ***Focus the lesson*** on note values. Use the musical pizzas to explain whole notes, half notes, and quarter notes. Have the students count the number of whole notes, half notes, and quarter notes in *Fantasie-Impromptu*. You may want to have the pizzas increased in size.
4. ***Activity:*** Using the Note Value Cards, explain that a whole note receives 4 counts, a half note 2 counts, and a quarter note 1 count. Raise each card and ask: "What is the name of this note?" and "How many beats does it get?"
5. ***Activity:*** Reproduce enough copies of the Note Value Cards Page for each student. Cut out the cards and place them in a pack for each student. Ask the students to raise the correct card in response to the questions: "Which note is a whole note?" and "Which note receives four counts?" Ask these questions about each note value. Mix them up!

Activity Page: The students should place the correct note, count, and word from the topping menu on the corresponding pizza cut.

Story of *Fantasie-Impromptu*

Chopin was regarded as the "Poet of the Piano." He was a man of Polish and French blood who spent most of his career in Paris, France. The greatest part of his music was composed exclusively for the piano. As the piano became more advanced and perfected, Chopin was able to expand his potential in composing for it. The *Fantasie-Impromptu* was never published during Chopin's lifetime, and he wanted it and other pieces destroyed so the public wouldn't hear these works before they were completely ready.

However, Chopin wasn't always so serious and concerned about great composing. Once a friend, whom Chopin was visiting, had a little dog that would incessantly run around and around in a circle chasing its tail. Chopin and his friend would sit and chuckle while being entertained by this little pooch. The friend suggested to Chopin that he write a piece of music about the dog. So he did, and called it "Waltz for a Little Dog."

Musical Excerpt
from *Fantasie-Impromptu*
FREDERIC CHOPIN (1810–1849)

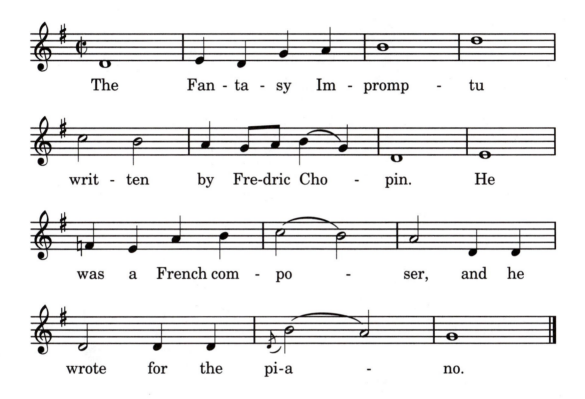

The Fan - ta - sy Im - promp - tu writ - ten by Fre-dric Cho - pin. He was a French com - po - ser, and he wrote for the pi-a - no.

Music Pizzas Page

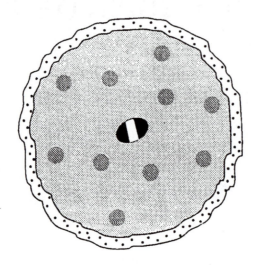

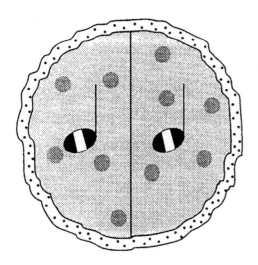

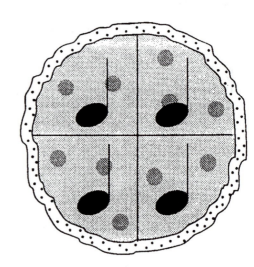

Note Value Cards Page

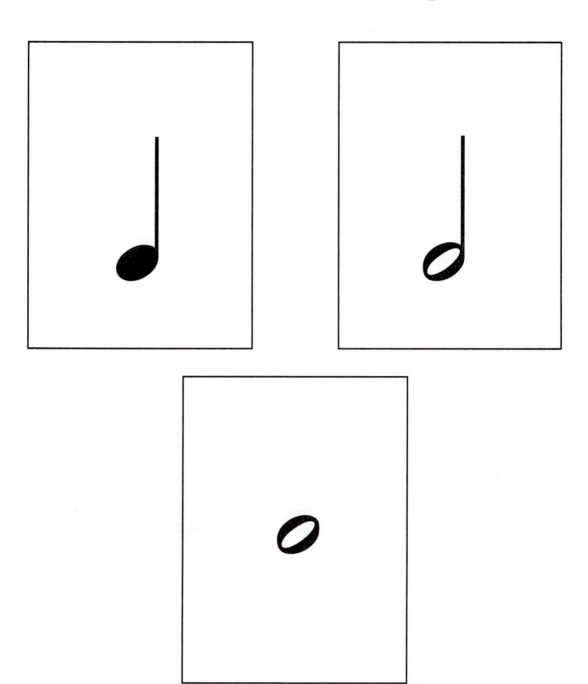

Note Values Activity Page

Music Pizzas

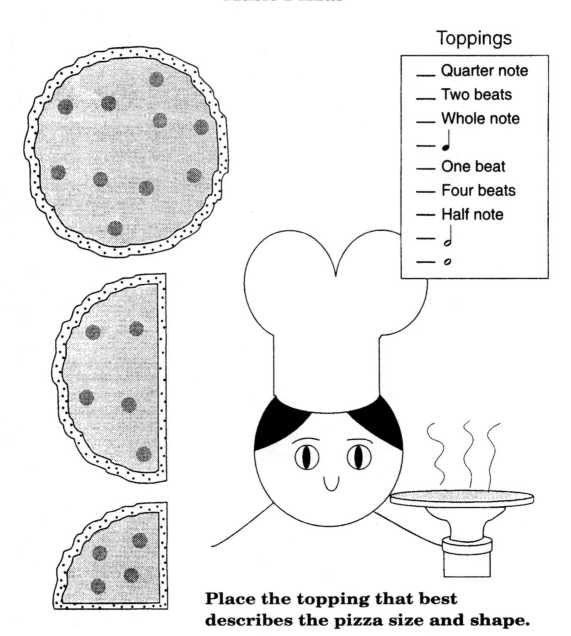

Toppings

___ Quarter note
___ Two beats
___ Whole note
___ ♩
___ One beat
___ Four beats
___ Half note
___ ♪
___ 𝅝

Place the topping that best describes the pizza size and shape.

Largo
(DVORAK)

Lesson Plan

Objective: Students will define and perform the tempo of largo.

Materials: Piano
                    Copies of the Largo Activity Page
                    Copies of the Music Crossword Puzzle

Procedure: 1. ***Tell the story*** of *Largo* to the students.

                    2. ***Teach the tune*** to the students. You may want to copy the tune
                       for each student or use an overhead projector to allow students
                       to sing it with the piano (p) marking at the beginning as a re-
                       view.

                    3. ***Focus the lesson*** on the tempo and the term largo. Define the
                       term as meaning slow and/or broad. Make a comparison with
                       adagio. Perhaps have the students think of the term adagio first,
                       and then largo.

                    4. ***Activity:*** Put students into groups. Have them come up with
                       things that are slow and things that are very slow. Use the ac-
                       tivity page for students to record their responses.

Activity Page: Use this page for the students to write down their examples of
                    things that are slow (adagio) and things that are very slow (largo).

Music Crossword Puzzle: Have the students use the term bank to help them com-
                    plete the puzzle.

Story of *Largo*

Largo comes from a larger work called the *Ninth Symphony*, or the *New World Symphony*, by Dvorak. He was a Czechoslovakian composer who came to America in 1892 to become the director of the National Conservatory of Music in New York. He wanted to write a piece of music that recorded a visitor's viewpoint of the vast new land called America. Being a folk composer, he also wished to depict the spirit of African-American folk music. The folksong that Dvorak bases the second movement on is the old American folktune "Going Home."

While in America, Dvorak missed being able to take part in his passionate hobbies of pigeons and locomotives (trains). A friend of his tried to help him by taking him to the New York City Zoo to see the pigeon display. But, it was more of a problem to arrange to see locomotives. The train station authorities were not willing to allow anyone near the trains who did not have a ticket or was not going on a trip. Unfortunately, the only other place to see trains was along the river, but you could only see them from a distance. However, it was worth it because Dvorak saw a steamship for the first time, and steamships became a new passionate hobby for him.

Musical Excerpt from *"Largo"*
New World Symphony No: 9
ANTON DVORAK (1841—1904)

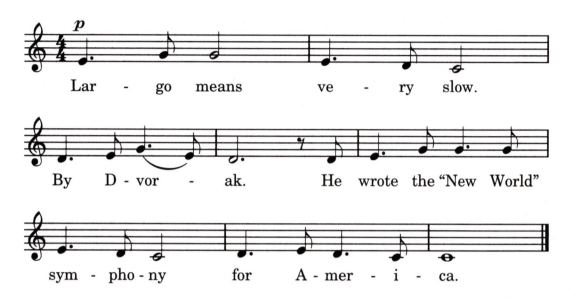

Lar - go means ve - ry slow.

By D - vor - ak. He wrote the "New World"

sym - pho - ny for A - mer - i - ca.

Largo Activity Page

List things that are slow (adagio) and things that are very slow (largo).

LARGO	ADAGIO

Music Crossword Puzzle

DOWN

1. Forte means this.
2. Chopin wrote for this instrument.
4. A brass instrument
6. A round is a type of this form.

ACROSS

3. Slow
5. Very slow
7. Music and dance form
8. Soft/quiet

Music Crossword Puzzle Answer Key

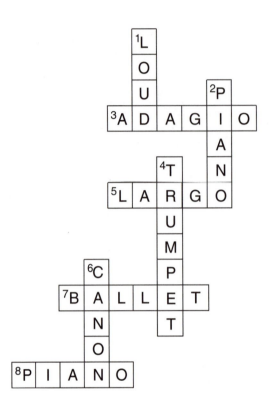

DOWN

1. Forte means this.
2. Chopin wrote for this instrument.
4. A brass instrument
6. A round is a type of this form.

ACROSS

3. Slow
5. Very slow
7. Music and dance form
8. Soft/quiet

Classic Tunes & Tales Composers
Wordsearch No. 1

P	S	Y	U	D	R	S	J	C	A	V	U	W	P	T	I	L	U	P	O
E	E	K	M	V	O	C	R	Z	K	Q	G	D	A	C	U	T	G	I	W
I	Y	M	V	O	S	H	P	B	S	D	K	P	C	H	Z	Z	A	Q	M
B	V	R	D	R	S	U	R	M	N	O	P	P	H	A	I	R	Y	G	B
X	R	I	K	A	I	M	W	T	U	T	T	D	E	I	J	X	G	H	P
Q	R	A	N	K	N	A	Z	O	P	U	D	M	L	K	E	U	Y	R	B
B	B	B	H	C	I	N	C	S	C	Q	G	H	B	O	Z	R	A	P	Q
C	E	Q	A	M	W	N	D	H	G	O	T	D	E	V	K	H	P	U	K
H	B	E	C	C	S	C	L	A	R	K	E	N	L	S	S	X	Q	Y	H
O	M	S	T	F	H	Z	H	H	H	R	C	S	R	K	N	J	G	Q	H
P	B	O	N	H	X	X	W	R	A	T	L	O	C	Y	K	Q	J	C	D
I	C	M	Z	R	O	K	U	S	Z	Y	G	V	C	H	L	P	H	O	Q
N	J	O	A	A	J	V	N	S	T	U	D	H	V	N	U	U	L	W	R
I	C	Z	P	E	R	R	E	F	I	P	V	N	I	P	E	B	V	R	J
K	O	H	Z	L	D	T	P	N	U	K	K	P	W	I	I	E	E	R	P
G	J	I	H	T	A	R	A	C	H	M	A	N	I	N	O	F	F	R	M
L	R	U	A	F	K	N	P	S	T	R	A	V	I	N	S	K	Y	B	T
S	B	I	V	U	C	E	D	T	S	Z	Z	I	X	S	H	E	I	X	K
M	J	X	E	V	O	L	C	X	Q	P	E	P	A	R	K	F	S	H	Q
G	W	F	F	G	C	I	T	L	F	G	V	J	V	F	K	O	J	X	F

1. BACH
2. BEETHOVEN
3. BRAHMS
4. CHOPIN
5. CLARKE
6. COPLAND
7. DVORAK
8. GRIEG
9. HAYDN
10. MOZART
11. PACHELBEL
12. RACHMANINOFF
13. ROSSINI
14. SCHUBERT
15. SCHUMANN
16. STRAVINSKY
17. TCHAIKOVSKY

Classic Tunes & Tales Composers
Wordsearch No. 1
Answer Key

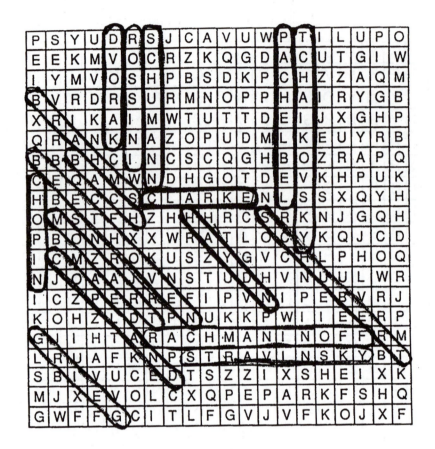

1. BACH
2. BEETHOVEN
3. BRAHMS
4. CHOPIN
5. CLARKE
6. COPLAND
7. DVORAK
8. GRIEG
9. HAYDN
10. MOZART
11. PACHELBEL
12. RACHMANINOFF
13. ROSSINI
14. SCHUBERT
15. SCHUMANN
16. STRAVINSKY
17. TCHAIKOVSKY

Classic Tunes Level II Test

Directions: Give each student a copy of the Level II Tunes Test Activity Page that follows. Instruct students to use the composer bank to match each title they hear you play with its composer. Then play each tune in its order. REMEMBER: The tune, title and composer are all interchangeable memory triggers.

TITLE

1. Fantasie-Impromptu
2. Rodeo
3. Largo
4. Canon in D
5. The Trout
6. Fifth Symphony
7. Trumpet Voluntary
8. Symphony No. 2
9. Happy Farmer
10. The Nutcracker

COMPOSER

Chopin
Copland
Dvorak
Pachelbel
Schubert
Beethoven
Clarke
Rachmaninoff
Schumann
Tchaikovsky

Composer Bank

Tchaikovsky	Clarke	Chopin
Copland	Beethoven	Rachmaninoff
Schubert	Dvorak	Schumann
Pachelbel		

Level II Tunes Test Activity Page

TITLE	COMPOSER
1. *Fantasie-Impromptu*	_____
2. *Rodeo*	_____
3. *Largo*	_____
4. *Canon in D*	_____
5. *The Trout*	_____
6. *Fifth Symphony*	_____
7. *Trumpet Voluntary*	_____
8. *Symphony No. 2*	_____
9. *Happy Farmer*	_____
10. *The Nutcracker*	_____

Composer Bank

Tchaikovsky	Clarke	Chopin
Copland	Beethoven	Rachmaninoff
Schubert	Dvorak	Schumann
Pachelbel		

LEVEL III:
(GRADE LEVELS: 3-4)

Hallelujah Chorus
(HANDEL)

Lesson Plan

Objective: Students will identify the tonal notation on the lines and spaces of the treble clef: E, G, B, D, F (lines) and F, A, C, E (spaces).

Materials: Piano
Chalkboard
Copies of the Letter Name Cards (cut and clasped)
Pencils
Copies of the Letter Names Activity Page
Copies of the Notation Activity Page

Procedure: 1. **Tell the story** of *Messiah* to the students. Define oratorio as a musical that tells a religious story.

2. **Teach the tune** to the students.

3. **Focus the lesson** on notation. Explain the lines and spaces on the staff. Use the sentence Every Good Boy Does Fine and the word FACE as mnemonic devices. Have the students use their hands (fingers as lines and spaces) to help them figure out note names. Use the Letter Name Cards. Copy enough for each student. Laminated oaktag would be a longer-lasting material. Punch holes in the cards and use a string or clasp to bind them together. As an activity, draw a staff and put a note on the board and have the students display the appropriate Letter Name Card.

4. **Game:** Divide the class into two teams, and have them stand. Place a note on the board, and have the first person on each team try to name the correct letter name. If they're incorrect, they should sit down. If they do answer it correctly, they remain standing. Rotate from person to person on each team. After going around the entire class, the team with the most people standing is the winner.

Activity Page: Instruct the students to write in the correct letter name below the notes on the Letter Names Activity Page.

Notation Activity Page: The student should draw the note on the correct line or space corresponding to the letter given. Have the students use the correct letters to complete the sentences and story. You may want to do the first example on the board with the students.

Added Lesson: Have the students circle the quarter rests on the Letter Names Activity Page.

Answer Key: Letter Names Activity Page
d, a, b, a, d, a, b, a, a, b, a, a, b, a, a, g, f, e, e, f

Story of the *Hallelujah Chorus*

The *Hallelujah Chorus* was the final piece of the second part in the grand oratorio called the *Messiah*. Handel composed it in twenty-four days. When Handel had finished the work, it has been said that his servant found him with tears streaming down his face because he felt that he had really seen heaven. The first performance was a charity for hospitals and prisoners; it was the year 1742. The libretto, or text (words/story), of the music dealt with the beginning, the suffering, and the faith of Christianity. The *Hallelujah Chorus* is a joyful celebration of his religion and his strongly held faith.

One Sunday, Handel was attending a friend's church. When the service ended, Handel asked the organist of the church if he could play the postlude (music as the congregation leaves the church). The organist said "Sure! You can play them out." With his mastery of the organ, Handel captivated the people, and they remained in their seats. The organist was growing impatient with Handel because he was anxious to leave. After stewing awhile, the organist blurted out to Handel: "You better stop. I was wrong. You can't play them out. They won't move!"

Musical Excerpt
from *Hallelujah Chorus*
GEORGE FRIEDRICH HÄNDEL
(1685–1759)

Hal - le - lu - jah! Han - del's mu - sic; He called it Mes - si - ah, an or - a - tor - i - o.

Letter Name Cards Page

A

B

C

D

E

F

G

Letter Names Activity Page

Place the correct letter names under each note.

Name _____

Notation Activity Page

Using whole notes (**O**), place the note on the correct line or space.

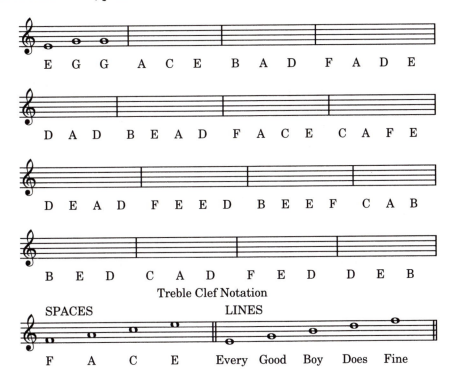

E G G   A C E   B A D   F A D E

D A D   B E A D   F A C E   C A F E

D E A D   F E E D   B E E F   C A B

B E D   C A D   F E D   D E B

Treble Clef Notation

SPACES   LINES

F   A   C   E   Every Good Boy Does Fine

Fill in the words that match the notes on the staff to complete the sentence.

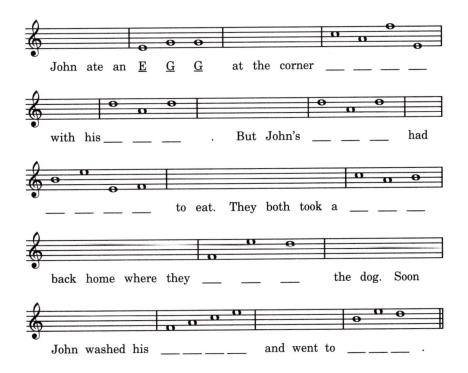

John ate an <u>E</u> <u>G</u> <u>G</u> at the corner __ __ __ __

with his __ __ __ .   But John's __ __ __ had

__ __ __ __ to eat.   They both took a __ __ __

back home where they __ __ __ the dog.   Soon

John washed his __ __ __ __ and went to __ __ __ .

The Four Seasons
(VIVALDI)

Lesson Plan

Objective: The students will learn to recognize the tempo "allegro" and the terms "ritardando" and "a tempo."

Materials: Piano
Copies of the Tempo Pages
Copies of Ritardando/A Tempo Activity Page

Procedure:

1. *Tell the story* of *The Four Seasons* to the students.
2. *Teach the tune* to the students.
3. *Focus the lesson* on the tempo allegro and the terms ritardando and a tempo.
4. *Activity:* Sing "Yankee Doodle" and have the students run in place for allegro and gradually slow down when you raise the word ritardando. Use the word a tempo to have the students resume their tempo of allegro. Try this with various songs. Also, try having the students sing while flashing the ritardando and a tempo cards.
5. *Activity:* Ask the students to wiggle or twist their torsos when you say the word allegro. Have them gradually slow down when you display the word ritardando. They will return to the allegro movement when you display the word a tempo.

Activity Page: Have the students write in ritardando (rit. or ritard) where the car has to slow down and a tempo where it resumes its speed.

Mnemonic Device: Use the allegro "A Leg Grows Fast" mnemonic to help students remember what allegro means.

Answer Key: Ritardando/A Tempo Activity Page
A Tempo, Ritardando, Ritardando, Ritardando, A Tempo, Ritardando

Story of *The Four Seasons*

Vivaldi was born in Venice, Italy, about 1676. He spent most of his career as the music director for a girl's orphanage. However, he began in the profession of a priest, nicknamed the "Red Priest" because of his red hair. But, due to his asthmatic problems, he was released. Fortunately for the music world, he became one of the most prolific concerto composers of his day—writing hundreds of them. Subsequently, only 85 concertos were published. Twelve of his most famous concertos were *The Four Seasons*—Spring, Summer, Autumn, and Winter—published in 1725. In these concertos, the violin is highlighted, most likely because Vivaldi helped make the Italian School of Violin famous and well respected.

The "Red Priest," as Vivaldi was known, once said the mass service, and suddenly thought of a theme for a piece of music. He ran out of the sanctuary to a chamber down the hall and wrote out the music. The church officials were quite astounded and so furious about his peculiar actions that they expressed their disappointment quite clearly. However, that was about all the punishment they felt they could bestow on the musical genius. But, they decided that was the last mass he would do.

Musical Excerpt
from *The Four Seasons*
"The Spring"
ANTONIO VIVALDI (1676–1741)

Allegro

The Four Sea-sons are here. Vi - val-di's sound is _ clear. The

Spring is the first you hear. It's fol - lowed by each sea - son for

which there is a rea-son. It's time for Bar-oque style of mu - sic.

Ritardando Page

RITARDANDO

A Tempo Page

A TEMPO

Allegro Page

A leg grows *FAST*

Ritardando/A Tempo Activity Page

Write in *ritardando* where the car has to gradually slow down and *a tempo* where it goes back to allegro (fast). Use the spaces given below.

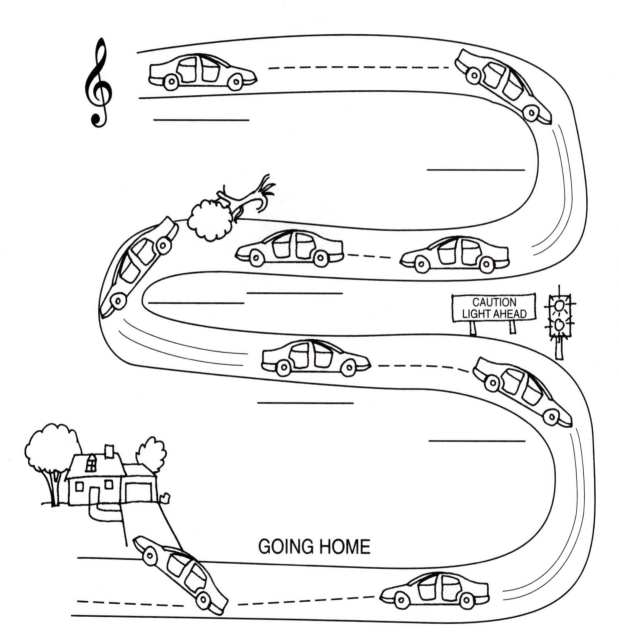

CAUTION
LIGHT AHEAD

GOING HOME

Rigoletto
(VERDI)

Lesson Plan

Objective: Students will identify and perform the term and tempo of moderato.

Materials: Piano
Copies of the Tempo Cards made from the *Rigoletto* Activity Page
Empty container
Hand drums

Procedure: 1. ***Tell the story*** of *Rigoletto* to the students.

2. ***Teach the tune*** to the students.

3. ***Focus the lesson*** on the tempo of the tune—moderato.

4. ***Review*** the tempos adagio, largo, moderato, and allegro.

5. ***Activity:*** Find a safe area where the students can run. Then put numerous tempo cards in a container. Select from largo, adagio, moderato, and allegro. Have the students pick a card and walk very slow for largo, walk slowly for adagio, jog for moderato, and run for allegro. Make a large sign with *a tempo* and one with *ritardando* printed on them. Raise the signs off and on while the students move to their chosen tempos within the selected area.

6. ***Activity:*** Ask the students to name tunes that could be identified as moderato, and then sing the tunes. Also, review tunes that are adagio, allegro, and largo.

7. ***Extended activity:*** Have the students clap, tap, or drum (using a hand drum) the beat of the tunes from above.

Activity Page: Copy, cut, and laminate the Tempo Cards on the *Rigoletto* Activity Page for the lesson activity.

Story of *Rigoletto*

Rigoletto is a hunchbacked jester in the court of a duke and duchess. The duke is a man who loves to win the affections of any lady he wants. One day the duke orders that a count be executed because the count had attacked the duke for trying to take his daughter. In response, the count puts a curse on Rigoletto.

Many people poked fun at Rigoletto, perhaps because he kept a girl locked up in his chamber. They believed the girl was his girlfriend, but she was actually his daughter. Rigoletto tried to conceal her from his boss, the duke. But unfortunately, the duke finds out about her, and Rigoletto decides to have the duke kidnapped and hauled away, far away, so as not to be seen ever again. Consequently, the same people who made fun of Rigoletto decide to play a joke on the disadvantaged jester by stealing his girl from his room and placing her in the duke's chamber for Rigoletto to discover. So Rigoletto moves into the duke's chamber and ties the duke up and puts him in a sack so that the hired kidnapper can carry him off easily. The count's men, playing a joke on Rigoletto, bring Gilda, Rigoletto's daughter, in a sack to the duke's quarters. The hired kidnapper takes Gilda mistakenly and carries her off, never to be seen again. Once he realized what has happened, Rigoletto becomes overcome with grief, believing that the executed count's curse has succeeded.

Musical Excerpt from *Rigoletto*
La Donna é Mobile
GIUSEPPI VERDI (1813–1901)

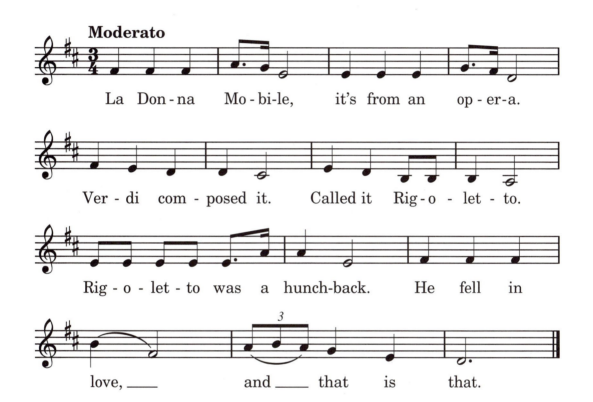

LARGO

ADAGIO

MODERATO

ALLEGRO

Can-Can
(OFFENBACH)

Lesson Plan

Objective: The students will identify the tempo of presto.

Materials: Piano
Copies of the Presto Card Page
Copies of the Presto Activity Page

Procedure:
1. *Tell the story* of *Can-Can* to the students.
2. *Teach the tune* to the students.
3. *Focus the lesson* on the presto tempo.
4. *Game:* Have the students form a circle. Choose one student to close their eyes and stand in the center of the circle. Give the Presto Card to another student to hide. Have the students run around the circle while singing the tune. After the tune is over, have the students stop. The student in the center will run inside the circle and point and yell "presto" at three students to try to find who has the card. If he/she guesses correctly, they go on again; if not, the one with the card goes to the center.
5. *Activity:* Using words such as: turtle, jet, lightning, molasses, etc., call out a word to the students. Have them say "presto" if the word fits the tempo, or "not" if it doesn't.
6. *Follow-up activity:* Use the same activity as above, but use tunes instead of words.

Activity Page: Have the students put the names of the pictures and words on the lines.

Story of *Can-Can*

Gaite Parisenne is a ballet that takes place in a cafe where a ball is held every evening. Dancing around the cafe are girl attendants. Most prominent are the very pretty young flowergirl and an intriguing glove-seller. There are many wealthy people in attendance at the cafe. A young Austrian baron notices the glove-seller, thus invoking the jealousy of the flowergirl. Shortly, the baron and an army officer quarrel because they both are fascinated by the glove-seller. As the two men calm down, a floor show of dancing begins and all take part in the evening festivities.

By the end of the evening the stage clears, and the baron and the glove-seller fall in love. The officer, alone and sad, storms off the stage.

The day Offenbach died, a friend arrived at the composer's home and said to the servant, "How is he?" The servant replied: "Mr. Offenbach is dead. He died peacefully, and he didn't know it." The friend said, jokingly, "Just wait till he finds out!"

Musical Excerpt from *Can-Can*
(Gaité Parisenne)
JACQUES OFFENBACH (1819–1880)

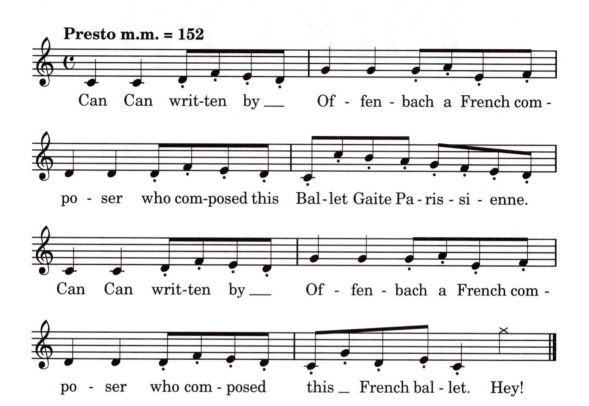

Presto m.m. = 152

Can Can writ-ten by __ Of - fen - bach a French com -

po - ser who com-posed this Bal-let Gaite Pa - ris - si - enne.

Can Can writ-ten by __ Of - fen - bach a French com -

po - ser who com - posed this __ French bal - let. Hey!

Presto Card Page

PRESTO

Presto Activity Page

Write the names of all the things in the magician's hat that would occur **"presto"-change-o** quick.

_____   _____

_____   _____

_____   _____

Concerto in E Minor
(MENDELSSOHN)

Lesson Plan

Objective: Students will identify the term concerto.

Materials: Piano
Drum
Rhythm sticks
Recording of a concerto (soloist and orchestra)
Copies of the Concerto Activity Page

Procedure:
1. ***Tell the story*** of *Concerto in E minor* to the students.
2. ***Teach the tune*** to the students.
3. ***Explain*** the definition of a concerto to the students: a concerto is generally a large-scale work, like a symphony, which highlights a solo instrument with an orchestra. Also, define tutti as the time when everybody plays together at the same time, and cadenza as the section that features the soloist alone.
4. ***Focus the lesson*** on the concerto. Ask the students to name an an instrument they might see as the soloist in a concerto.
5. ***Listening activity:*** Play a recording of a concerto. Have the students raise their hand when they hear the solo instrument.

Activity Page: Have one student play a drum and the rest of the class rhythm sticks while performing the Concerto for Drum. You may substitute instruments for the concerto.

Level III Quiz: Have students complete the Level III Quiz on page 142 for a quick review of tempo terms and compositions. Answers to the first part: 1. e, 2. d, 3. b, 4. a, 5. e.

Story of *Concerto in E Minor*

Felix Mendelssohn was born in Germany, the son and grandson of a family of intellectuals. He organized, arranged, directed, performed, and composed music during his very short career. Following a successful tour of England, he returned to Germany suffering from nervous exhaustion. Soon, thereafter he received a severe blow: his sister, whom he was very fond of, died. Months later, Mendelssohn himself died of a stroke.

Concerto in E Minor was written for violin and orchestra. It was intended to be a "show off" piece—showing off a great performer (virtuoso). When Mendelssohn wrote this concerto, he had a particular musician in mind—a friend who played violin in an orchestra. Mendelssohn wrote his friend and told him that he had a tune running through his head, leaving him no peace. And with much advice from his friend, Mendelssohn completed this work by 1844.

Mendelssohn once received a visitor while he was sitting and writing music at a table. The visitor began to walk quietly out of the room, but Mendelssohn, politely asked him to stay. "Don't worry, I'm just copying," the composer said. The visitor noticed no other papers, no thinking, and no humming. After a long visit and conversation, the visitor realized that Mendelssohn knew his music so well he could copy it without any written or singing assistance.

Musical Excerpt
from *Concerto in E Minor*
FELIX MENDELSSOHN (1809–1847)

Allegro molto appasionato

p

This mu - sic, this mu - sic by Fe - lix Men-dels-sohn. For

vi - o __ lin and or - che-stra. He named it con-cer - to.   A

Ger - man com - po - ser in nine-teenth cen - tur - y.   He

lived such a short life thir-ty-eight years old   Fe-lix Men-dels-sohn.

Concerto Activity Page

Concerto for Drum

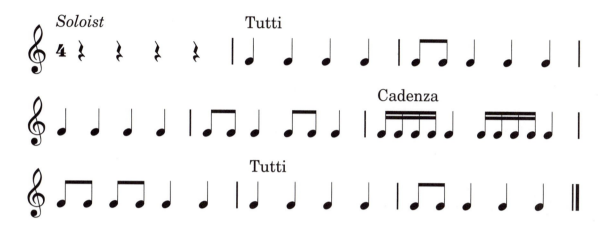

Orchestra of Sticks

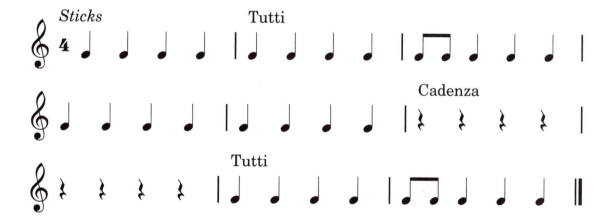

Classic Tunes Level III Quiz

I. Matching

Directions: Draw a line to the tempo that matches the definition.

Definition   **Tempo**

1. Medium speed   a. Largo

2. Slowly   b. Allegro

3. Fast and lively   c. Presto

4. Very slow and broad   d. Adagio

5. Extremely fast and quick   e. Moderato

II. Listening

Directions: After listening to the tune, chose the correct title of the tune, and place it on the correct numberline in the order you hear each.

1. _____   *Concerto in E Minor*

2. _____   *Hallelujah Chorus*

3. _____   *Can-Can*

4. _____   *Rigoletto*

5. _____   *The Four Seasons*

Toreador Song
(BIZET)

Lesson Plan

Objective: Students will recognize 4/4 meter (time signature).

Materials: Piano
Copies of Meter Cards made from Meter Cards Page
Chalkboard
Copies of the Meter/Time Signature Activity Page

Procedure: 1. ***Tell the story*** of *Toreador Song* to the students.

2. ***Teach the tune*** to the students.

3. ***Focus the lesson*** on meter. The tune is in common time. Explain common time to mean the same as 4/4 meter. The meter tells how long one stays in a measure and what note equals one beat for counting the time. Use the Meter Cards to teach the lesson. The odd-shaped 4 is the Note Value Number Card. Give examples of the activity page on the chalkboard.

   Another suggestion: make 9 x 12 oaktag cards with quarter notes, half notes, eighth notes, sixteenth notes, and their rests. Choose a few students to form four to eight measures of two then four beats per bar.

4. ***Activity:*** After placing the examples below on the board, have the students clap or use sticks to the rhythm. Have the students write the beat number under each note.

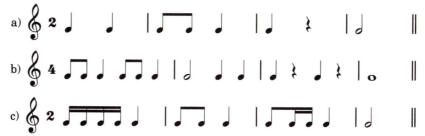

Have the students count as they perform. Use tah (♩), tah-ah (♩), tah-ah-ah-ah (o), ti-ti (♫), ti-ka-ti-ka (♬), and ti—ti-ka (♫).

Activity Page: First, the students are to fill in the correct number for each missing meter exercise. For the second half, students will circle the measure that does not correspond with the given meter.

Answer Key: Meter/Time Signature Activity Page
3, 2, 4; 2nd measure, 3rd measure. 3rd measure.

Story of the *Toreador Song*

In Spain, about 1820, there was a gypsy girl named Carmen, who meets a soldier, Jose, by throwing a flower at his feet. At first, he pays no attention to her. But soon he becomes interested in her reckless charm. Another girl comes to Jose telling him that his mother wishes him to marry another girl and return to his mother. Later, Carmen gets arrested for injuring a fellow worker at the factory, and Jose is ordered to guard her as he escorts her to prison. However, with her persuasive approach and charm, Carmen convinces Jose to set her free. Carmen flees to an inn where she dances with friends. A famous bullfighter wants to dance with Carmen, but she is waiting for Jose to return from jail—where he was placed for letting her escape. After Jose arrives, the captain of the army insists that Jose return to his barracks, but Jose refuses. So Jose and Carmen run off to the mountains. The bullfighter comes to fight Jose for Carmen, and the girl Jose's mother wanted him to marry comes to tell him to return to his mother, for she is dying. Jose does go home, and Carmen then becomes enchanted with the bullfighter and joins him on his way to the bullring. However, she finds out that Jose is on his way. They quarrel, and she refuses to go off with him as she throws the ring he gave to her at his feet. In the background, the roar of the crowd cheering the bullfighter can be heard.

Musical Excerpt
from the *Toreador Song* (Carmen)
GEORGE BIZET (1838–1875)

Tor - e - a-dor Song writ-ten by Bi-zet.   From an o - per-a

Car-men was its name.   Takes place in the nine-teenth cen-tu-ry

Spain's bull-fight-er es - ca-pade.   A sol-dier falls in love

and Car-men, too.   A tra-gic op - er - a.

Meter Cards Page

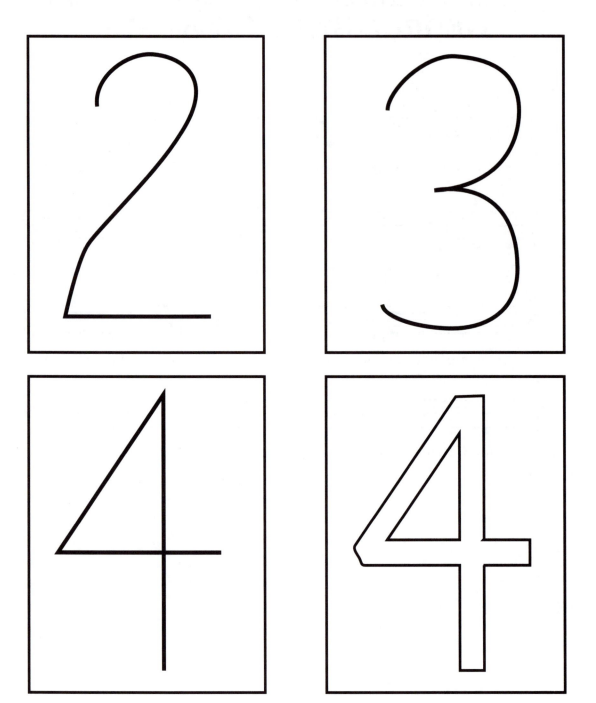

Meter/Time Signature Activity Page

Example of 2/4 Meter

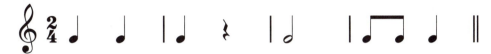

Fill in the correct beats per measure of the meter for each exercise.

Circle the incorrect measure of each meter exercise.

Stars and Stripes Forever
(SOUSA)

Lesson Plan

Objective: Students will recognize and identify a sharp (#).

Materials: Piano
                        Tone bells
                        Music books
                        Sharp cards from Sharp-Flat-Natural Cards Page
                        Copies of the Sharps Activity Page

Procedure: 1. *Tell the story* of *Stars and Stripes* to the students.

                        2. *Teach the tune* to the students.

                        3. *Focus the lesson* on the sharp. Point out to the students that a sharp makes a note sound higher. "If you sit on something sharp, you'll go up." It is the same with a sharp in music.

                        4. *Demonstrate*: Play a few natural pitches on the piano, then play its sharp. Help students hear the higher pitch. Try a few more on the piano or on tone bells.

                        5. *Activity:* Play a number of natural pitches. If the note goes up, have the students put their thumbs up. If the note stays the same, have them turn their thumbs point at one another.

                        6. *Activity:* Give each student a music book or music textbook. Pick a song or exercise, and ask students if it has a sharp in the song. Then, have the students find and discover songs that contain sharps.

Activity Page: The students are to circle all the sharps.

Story of *Stars and Stripes Forever*

John Phillip Sousa was born in 1854 in Washington, D.C. As a teenager, he played in the U.S. Marine Corps Band, and he eventually became its greatest and most famous conductor. To this day Sousa is considered " The March King," and rightfully so, for he had composed 136 marches. One of his most famous ones is *Stars and Stripes Forever*, which he composed upon a steamship while returning from a vacation in Italy in 1896. It has been said that he paced the deck of the ship a hundred times while trying to work out the music until it was just right.

Sousa was also known for suggesting the bell design of the "sousaphone." The sousaphone is a marching tuba. The typical tuba's bell points straight up, but the sousaphone's bell is curved and bent forward. It is an easier tuba to carry and the sound travels more directly ahead; ideal for marching. An interesting note: the Ohio State University band spells out the word "Ohio" during its field show, and the sousaphone player dots the "i."

Musical Excerpt
from *Stars and Stripes Forever*
JOHN PHILLIP SOUSA (1854–1932)

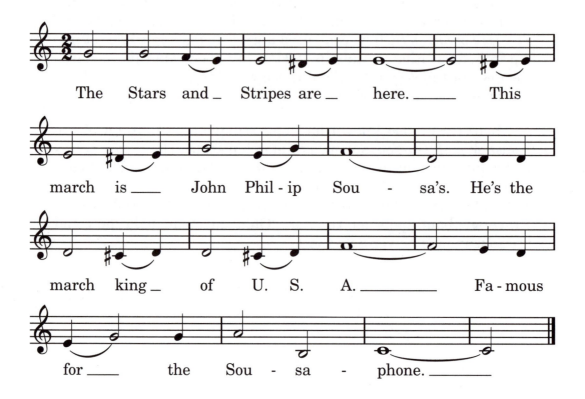

The Stars and _ Stripes are _ here. _____ This
march is ___ John Phil - ip Sou - sa's. He's the
march king _ of U. S. A. _____ Fa - mous
for ___ the Sou - sa - phone. _____

Sharp-Flat-Natural Cards Page

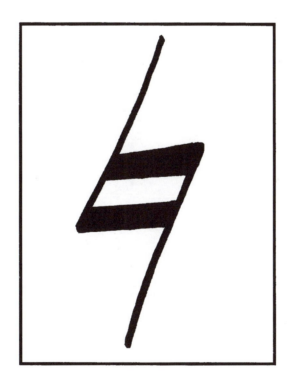

Sharps Activity Page

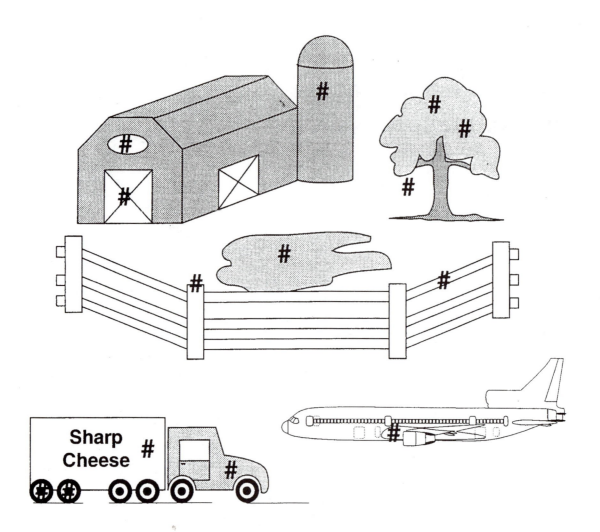

© 1997 by Parker Publishing Company

Try a Sharp Tic-Tac-Toe!

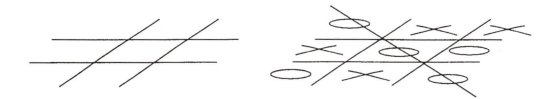

Scheherazade (RIMSKY-KORSAKOV)

Lesson Plan

Objective: The students will demonstrate a sharp on a keyboard.

Materials: Piano
Copies of the Keyboard Activity Page
Xylophone or bells
9 x 12 or 8.5 x 11 paper
Pencils

Procedure:
1. ***Tell the story*** of *Scheherazade* to the students.
2. ***Teach the tune*** to the students.
3. ***Focus the lesson*** on playing the sharp on the keyboard. This lesson will require doing the activity page first.
4. ***Activity page:*** Lead the students through the process of making a one-octave keyboard (or, you may use an already-made keyboard); however, students value this lesson much more when they produce their own work.
5. ***Activity:*** Explain how you move a halfstep on the keyboard. Be sure the students realize a sharp is a halfstep move upward to the right on the keyboard. Give the students a letter and ask them to find its sharp. Use C, D, F, G, and A first, and then use E and B when the students have mastered the others. Finally, Put a note on the board. Ask the students to find it on the keyboard.
6. ***Activity:*** This activity is an application activity. While using their keyboards, have the students play the following notes and its sharps.

   Place the following exercises on the board:

   *Possibly, have the students try these exercises on a real keyboard or set of bells.
7. ***Keep the keyboards*** for the next tune and activity.

Story of *Scheherazade*

Scheherazade is related to the story of how the tales in The Arabian Nights, or The Thousand and One Nights, were first told.

The story is about a sultan who had each new wife of his (as we remember, sultans sometimes had many wives) exiled to a deserted island after the first day of marriage because he thought all women were not trustworthy. One day, he married Scheherazade. On the first night of their marriage, she began telling the sultan a wonderful tale. He became so curious to hear more that he put off her exile for the next night. She cleverly continued with the tales and told stories of adventure and magic so skillfully that, after a thousand and one nights, the sultan gave up his plan to exile her.

The stories featured in Rimsky-Korsakov's tone poem are "The Sea and Sinbad's Ship," "The Story of the Kalendar Prince" (the Kalendars were wanderers who took a vow of poverty), "The Young Prince" and the "Young Princess" (a young couple falling in love), and "Festival at Bagdad," "The Sea," "The Ship Goes to Pieces Against the Rock Surrounded by a Bronze Warrior" (a festival and all its wonders is mysteriously transported onto a ship being thrown around in the story sea. A huge rock draws the ship towards the rock, and the rock brings the ship to its demise).

Musical Excerpt from *Scheherazade*
NICHOLAS RIMSKY-KORSAKOV
(1844–1908)

Rim-sky - Kor - sa-kov.   Rim-sky - Kor - sa-kov.   Wrote Sche-

her - a-zade   as   a   Rus - sian. Na-vy   Ad - mir - al   he   was.

And Sche - her - a - zade   told one   thou-sand tales   for one

thou-sand nights of A - ra - bi-a __ to her hus-band the mad sul-tan.

Keyboard Activity Page
(Teacher's Edition)

1. Draw a set of two goal posts and a set of three posts of the same size.

2. Draw a line to the left of the set of 2 and between both sets.

3. Draw 2 lines to the right of both sets.

4. Draw a line on the top and one on the bottom to connect the lines.

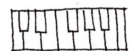

5. Write in the letters C,D,E,F,G,A,B, and C on the lower part of the keys.

6. Color the space black within the posts of each goal.

7. You may color the white keys, but use the light colors so you can read your letters.

© 1997 by Parker Publishing Company

Name _____

Keyboard Activity Page

1. Draw a set of two goal posts and a set of three posts of the same size.

2. Draw a line to the left of the set of 2 and between both sets.

3. Draw 2 lines to the right of both sets.

4. Draw a line on the top and one on the bottom to connect the lines.

5. Write in the letters C,D,E,F,G,A,B, and C on the lower part of the keys.

6. Color the space black within the posts of each goal.

7. You may color the white keys, but use the light colors so you can read your letters.

Till Eulenspiegel
(R. STRAUSS)

Lesson Plan

Objective: Students will identify the symbols flat (♭) and natural (♮).

Materials: Piano
Flat and natural cards
Copies of the Playing the Keyboard Activity Page

Procedure:
1. *Tell the story* of *Till Eulenspiegel* to the students.
2. *Teach the tune* to the students.
3. *Focus the lesson* on the flat and the natural. Use the flat and natural cards to help the students identify the symbols. Explain to the students: "If you flatten something, it goes down." To natural something is to return it to its normal state. Use the keyboards to try examples (the same as you did with the sharps) of flats. Also, show the students how to natural a note.
4. *Activity:* Have the students stand. Ask them to bend their knees and sit when you show a flat card and to stand normally when you display the natural card.
5. *Review* the sharp. Do the above activity. However, have the students jump or stretch when you show the sharp card. Do this activity numerous times.

Activity Page: Have the students use their keyboards to locate the letters and notes on the activity page.

Synthesis: Try using pianos or xylophones with the activity page. If you have a limited number of bells, keyboards, or xylophones, set up stations and put the students into teams that rotate from one station to the next.

Story of *Till Eulenspiegel*

Till was a lovable rogue of the fourteenth century who visited many cities and engaged in many occupations. He was a real-life person who rebelled against the establishment. Till remained, even after his death, a folklore figure known to all German children.

Till's escapades include riding a horse into the midst of a crowd of women in the market. He joins a group of priests, in disguise as one, and argues about theology while horrifying them with his disrespect. Till also declares his love for a damsel who gets tired of his antics. He shocks the Philistines by not playing by the rules, and proceeds by singing a fun street song. But as he observes the life about him, he experiences the loneliness of an outsider. Why can he not be like those around him and why can't he change? Till is Till, he believes he cannot change. Finally, he is brought to trial for his deeds, or mischievousness. He is no longer cocky, his luck has run out, and so has his time. He is found guilty—Till is no longer.

It is important to note how Richard Strauss put the story of *Till Eulenspiegel* into music. One can easily picture the antics and escapades of Till while listening to the tone poem. As a matter of fact, Strauss and a friend were having dinner at a popular New York City club when the two discussed how music can describe almost anything. Strauss insisted, "My friend, I could portray my knife, fork, and spoon being moved from one side of my plate to the other."

Musical Excerpt
from *Till Eulenspiegel*
RICHARD STRAUSS (1864–1949)

Till Eu-len-spie - gel. Till Eu-len-spie - gel. A mer-ry

prank-ster. Ger-man folk-lore boy mu-sic by Ri - chard

Strauss. Pro-blems here and trou-ble there.

Till was a great tone po - em by Strauss.

160

Name _____

Playing the Keyboard
Activity Page

Locate the key on your keyboard that corresponds with the letters below.

F   F♯   F♮ | E   E♭ | G   G♭   G♮ ‖

B   B♭ | B♯   B♮   B♭ | C♯   C♮ ‖

C♭   C♮ | A♯   A♭   A♮ | D   D♯   E♭ ‖

Play the following notes on your keyboard.

Try writing some of your own sharp, flat, and natural notes.

Symphonie-Fantastique
(BERLIOZ)

Lesson Plan

Objective: Students will identify and perform the articulations (slur, staccato, and legato).

Materials: Piano
Cards made from Articulation Cards Page
Copies of the Articulation Activity Page

Procedure: 1. ***Tell the story*** of *Symphonie-Fantastique* to the students.

2. ***Teach the tune*** to the students. Ask the students to notice how some syllables of the words have two or three notes connected and sung smoothly.

3. ***Focus the lesson*** on articulation. Demonstrate the differences between the slur, staccato, and legato. Use the Articulation Cards to show the students what each one looks like. Use the notes of B, A, and G on the piano, or any other instrument to demonstrate examples of each articulation.

4. ***Game:*** Have the students form a circle or remain seated. Choose one student to hide their eyes. Show the Articulation Cards in any order to all the circled students. Have them perform the articulations in groups of four quarter notes (i.e. ♩ ♩ ♩ ♩ | ♩ ♩ ♩ ♩ | ♩ ♩ ♩ ♩). ♩ = Dĭ ♩ = Dū ♩ ♩ = Dū-ū . The selected student should tiptoe when the class says staccato, walk for legato, and slide feet or fly using their arms as wings for the slur. If they are correct in the correct order, they pick the next student and next order of articulations.

Activity Page: Have the students perform the examples of articulation. First, have them say the syllables. Second, have them sing the syllables on any pitch or pitches. You may want to use the piano to assist.

Follow-Up: You may want to take previously learned tunes (i.e., *Surprise Symphony, Swan Lake*, and *Till*) for further examples of articulation. It may be interesting to sing some of the tunes in the opposite articulation as well as its original articulation. This would make a nice comparative activity.

Story of *Symphonie-Fantastique*

The Ball

Developed from his love of an actress, Berlioz composed a sort of autobiographical symphony called *Symphonie-Fantastique* in 1830. He wrote a letter to the actress explaining his feelings about her and the symphony, and invited her to the premiere of the new music; however, to his dismay, she didn't show.

The symphony's story begins with Berlioz making himself sick; however, he ends in a deep sleep accompanied by strange and mysterious visions, which he translates into music. The first segment, or movement, is called "Passions," in which he remembers the time before he fell in love. Then his intense love develops, and finally his return from love to his tenderness and religious fervor. The second movement is "A Ball." Berlioz finds his adored love at a ball (dance) during a celebration festival. The third movement is "Scene in the Countryside," in which he hears two shepherds calling one another in the fields where trees are swaying and leaves are rustling in a scene of tranquility. But his love appears again, and he is puzzled and unsure of her intentions. The sun sets and a distant thunder can be heard . . . for it is peaceful again. The fourth movement is "March to the Scaffold." His dream turns to a nightmare. His love is missing and he is thought to have killed her. The authorities sentence him to be hanged. The final movement is "Dream of a Witches' Sabbath," in which he believes he is in the middle of a witch's contrived crowd of hideous spirits, wizards, and monsters of every kind that have come to his hanging.

Musical Excerpt
from *Symphonie Fantastique*
"The Ball"
HECTOR BERLIOZ (1803–1869)

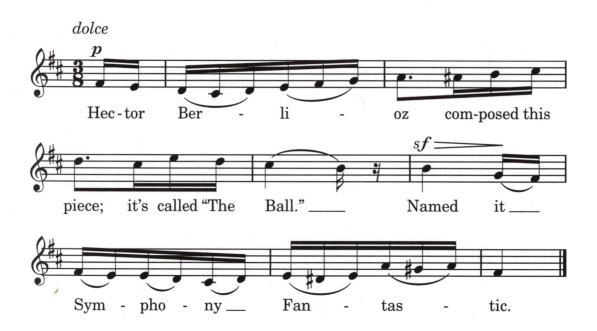

Hec-tor Ber - li - oz com-posed this piece; it's called "The Ball." ____ Named it ____ Sym - pho - ny ____ Fan - tas - tic.

Articulation Cards Page

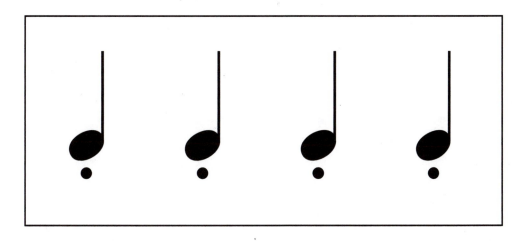

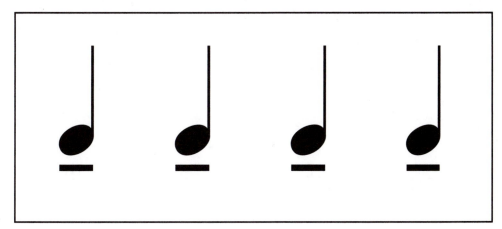

Articulation Activity Page

Sing the following exercises. First, say the articulation syllables. Second, sing on any pitch or pitches.

Staccato

Dĭ Dĭ Dĭ Dĭ   etc.

Legato

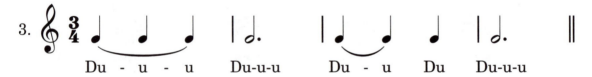

Dū Dū Dū   etc.

Slur

Du - u - u   Du-u-u   Du - u   Du   Du-u-u

Combined

Combined

5.

Name _____

Classic Tunes Level III Test

Listening: Put the titles of the tune in the order you hear them.

Tune Heard   *Titles*

1. _____   *Symphonie-Fantastique*

2. _____   *The Four Seasons*

3. _____   *Rigoletto*

4. _____   *Scheherazade*

5. _____   *Can-Can*

6. _____   *Till Eulenspiegel*

7. _____   *Concerto in E Minor*

8. _____   *Hallelujah Chorus*

9. _____   *Stars and Stripes Forever*

10. _____   *Toreador Song*

Matching: Match the title with the correct composer. Use the above titles.

1. Offenbach   _____

2. Rimsky-Korsakov   _____

3. Handel   _____

4. Richard Strauss   _____

5. Verdi   _____

6. Bizet   _____

7. Vivaldi   _____

8. Mendelssohn   _____

9. Sousa   _____

10. Berlioz   _____

LEVEL IV:
(GRADE LEVELS: 4-8)

Little Fugue in G Minor
(BACH)

Lesson Plan

Objective: Students will differentiate between Minor and Major tonalities.

Materials: Piano
Copies of the Major/Minor Cards Page
Copies of the Major/Minor Activity Page
Copies of the Major/Minor Tonality Listening Page

Procedure:
1. *Tell the story* of the Little Fugue to the students.
2. *Teach the tune* to the students.
3. *Question:* "Does it sound bright (happy) or dark (sad/cloudy)?
4. *Focus the lesson* on Major and Minor. Identify and play a few examples of Major and Minor triads. Play a few more examples and ask the students to identify them by thumbs up for Major and thumbs down for minor; thumbs in center for unsure.
5. *Activity:* Make enough copies of the Major/Minor Cards Page so each student has a set. Again, laminated oaktag works quite well. Play a variety of major and minor chords and tunes, and have the students raise the card that corresponds to the correct tonality. Additionally, ask each student to raise either a Major or Minor card—then play a chord or tune to each one.

Activity Page: Play the Classic Tunes and ask the students to fill in the correct modal key (Major or Minor). Adding chords to the melodies may help. Finally, have the students use their inner hearing to determine whether *William Tell Overture* is Major or minor—without hearing it played.

Additional Activity Page: Have the students sing a variety of tunes and songs. Write the titles on the board. Group the students into teams of 3 or 4 people. Ask them to categorize the tunes and songs into Major or Minor.

Answer Key: Major/Minor Activity Page
1. Major, 2. Minor, 3. Major, 4. Major, 5. Major, 6. Minor, 7. Major, 8. Major, 9. Major, 10. Minor.
William Tell Overture Major.

Story of *Little Fugue*

One of Bach's most popular pieces for organ was the *Little Fugue in G Minor*. The fugue was written for four voices. It starts with the subject (musical theme or tune) being announced by one voice, then developed in order by the other voices. The last voice produces a sort of flying song; that's why it's called a fugue (Latin for "flight"). As for the "G Minor" part of the "Little Fugue," traditionally the subject of a fugue is a Minor key.

Many musicians find the fugue a very complicated and difficult piece to perform. But, it is not known how the musicians of Bach's time felt about the fugue's difficulty. To Bach, it most likely didn't matter. Many musicians would ask Bach to compose a simple, easy piece for the harpsichord for them. With all good intentions, Bach would begin with a very simple theme or subject, but somehow would develop it into a very complicated work. When approached about the difficulty, Bach would reply, "You have ten healthy fingers as I do, so practice!"

Musical Excerpt
from *Little Fugue in G Minor*
J. S. BACH (1685–1750)

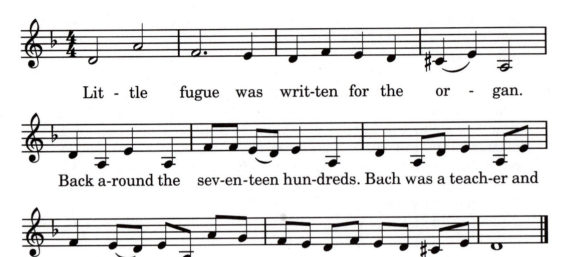

Lit - tle   fugue was   writ-ten for the   or - gan.

Back a-round the   sev-en-teen hun-dreds. Bach was a teach-er and

church comp-pos-er. He wrote lots of mu-sic we can hear to - day.

Major/Minor Cards Page

MAJOR

MINOR

Major/Minor Activity Page

All but three of the following tunes are in Major. Write in the correct key.

Tune   *Key (Major or Minor)*

1. *Eine Kleine Nacht Musik*   _____

2. *Swan Lake*   _____

3. *"Surprise" Symphony*   _____

4. *Can-Can*   _____

5. *Adagio*   _____

6. *Concerto for Violin*   _____

7. *Rigoletto*   _____

8. *Ode to Joy*   _____

9. *The Trout*   _____

10. *Symphony No. 40* (new!)   _____

Use your inner hearing for the tune below.

Is it Major or Minor?

William Tell Overture _____

Major/Minor Tonality Listening Page

Directions: Place the tunes, chords or songs you hear into the correct tonality categories.

Major	Minor

Emperor's String Quartet
(HAYDN)

Lesson Plan

Objective: Students will identify and perform the rhythm ♩. ♪.

Materials: Piano
Rhythm Sticks
Copy of Rhythm Card Page
Copies of the Rhythm Activity Page

Procedure: 1. ***Tell the story*** of the *Emperor's String Quartet* to the students.

2. ***Teach the tune*** to the students.

3. ***Echo clap*** the following rhythms with the students.

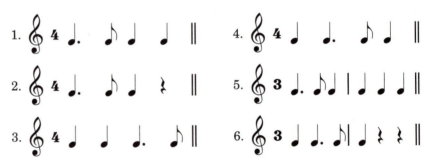

4. ***Focus the lesson*** on the ♩. ♪ rhythm. Teach the students how to count it ("tah-ee" or "1 2 and"). Display the Rhythm Card of ♩. ♪ .

5. ***Activity:*** Teach students to snap the sticks together on the quarter note and pull the joined sticks in a downward motion on the dotted-quarternote. Echo snap the *Emperor's String Quartet* tune, phrase by phrase. When the students know the tune well, have them snap the tune's entire rhythm while singing it, and then without singing.

Activity Page: Have the students sing the songs. Point out ♩. ♪ . After singing them once, have the students sing the song and clap on only the ♩. ♪ rhythm. Finally, have them write in the rhythms.

Follow-Up Activity: Using the songs and tunes on the activity page, play the songs in their entirety, and have the students use their rhythm sticks to play the rhythm to the song (possibly, use a recording of the songs). Perform these songs by memory or place them on an overhead projector.

Story of the *Emperor's String Quartet*

The *Emperor's String Quartet* was the popular name for Haydn's *String Quartet in C Major*, op. 76, No. 3. It was so named because the famous slow movement of the quartet was taken from the Emperor's Hymn, the Austrian national anthem (originally a solo song for voice and keyboard). Haydn was considered the father of the symphony, perhaps because he wrote over 100 symphonies. The Austrian composer spent time in Paris and London, where he had gained world recognition for his music. Besides symphonies, Haydn composed string quartets, concertos, and music for voice. He was a friend of Mozart and a teacher of Beethoven; nevertheless, his fame comes from his symphonic compositions.

Aside from having the passion to write beautiful music, Haydn also had a tendency to anger easily. While strolling with a musician friend down a street of Vienna, Haydn passed by an inn where musicians were playing a miserable rendition of one of his minuets. Haydn said to his friend "Let's go in," and his friend skeptically agreed. Haydn asked the fiddle player, "Who wrote this horrible minuet?" The fiddler, highly offended, jumped to his feet and poised for a fight. Fortunately Haydn's friend was a large man, and he got between the two angry men and shoved Haydn out the door.

Musical Excerpt
from *Emperor's String Quartet*
F. J. HAYDN (1732–1809)

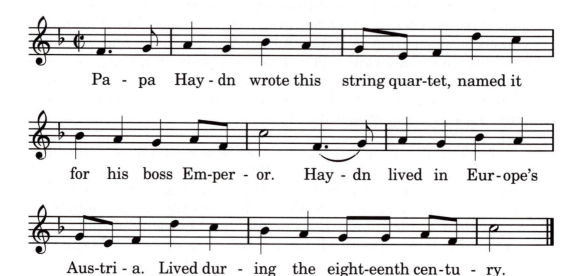

Pa - pa Hay - dn wrote this string quar-tet, named it

for his boss Em-per - or. Hay - dn lived in Eur-ope's

Aus-tri - a. Lived dur - ing the eight-eenth cen-tu - ry.

Rhythm Card Page

Rhythm Activity Page

Emperor's String Quartet

Pa - pa Hay - dn wrote this string quar - tet.

America

My coun - try 'tis of thee. Sweet land of li - ber - ty.

America, the Beautiful

Oh beau - ti - ful for spa - cious skies for am - ber waves of grain.

Eine Kleine Nacht Musik

Ei - ne Klei - ne Nacht Mu - sik.

Finlandia
(SIBELIUS)

Lesson Plan

Objective: The students will identify and perform the rhythm ⁷ ♪.

Materials: Piano
Rhythm Card Page
Copies of the Rhythm Activity Page

Procedure:
1. ***Tell the story*** of *Finlandia* to the students.

2. ***Teach the tune*** to the students.

3. ***Focus the lesson*** on ⁷ ♪. Explain that = , except for the rest on the beat. The rhythm may be counted as "rest-ti," "one an," or use your own method of count.

4. ***Echo clap*** the following exercises with the students. Try having the students stomp or take a breath on the rest.

5. ***Explain*** that the stomp is the (⁷) .

6. ***Activity:*** Put the following line of rhythms on the board:

Ask the students to clap and count each line. Then have them replace the ♫ rhythm with ⁷ ♪ . Follow up by counting and clapping the new rhythms. Proceed line to line.

Activity Page: The students count and clap the exercises. Also, have them fill in the missing measures using at least one ⁷ ♪ for each.

Additional Activity: Put the following line on the board.

Have the students move in place or in a circle. Ask them to step for each quarter note (♩), step and wait for two beats on the dotted-half note (♩.), step and jump for the focus rhythm (⁷ ♪), and wait for four beats when the whole note occurs (𝅝).

Story of *Finlandia*

Sibelius was a nationalist composer who was born in Finland the year the U.S. Civil War ended. In 1899, he composed a symphonic poem called *Finlandia*. The origin of *Finlandia* dates back to 1894 when the Russian Czar Nicholas II was tightening up his controlling rule of Finland. Political meetings were banned, but a number of charitable events were held to raise money for the Press Pension Fund without any sort of national theme. These events were called "press celebrations," or newspaper and magazine celebrations, and were intended to raise retirement money for people in the news media. One of these events consisted of a program or show of magazines and newspapers in which the history of Finland was portrayed. Sibelius composed *Finlandia* to accompany the press celebrations. His music stimulated a feeling of national pride in the Finns. Listening to Sibelius's work gave them a vivid picture of their country and its struggle for freedom.

In view of all the media attention and notoriety Sibelius was receiving for being a great composer, one of his students expressed some concerns about critics. Sibelius replied, with much visible displeasure, "Never pay any attention to what critics say. Remember, you'll never find a statue honoring a critic!"

© 1997 by Parker Publishing Company

Musical Excerpt from *Finlandia*
JAN SIBELIUS (1865–1957)

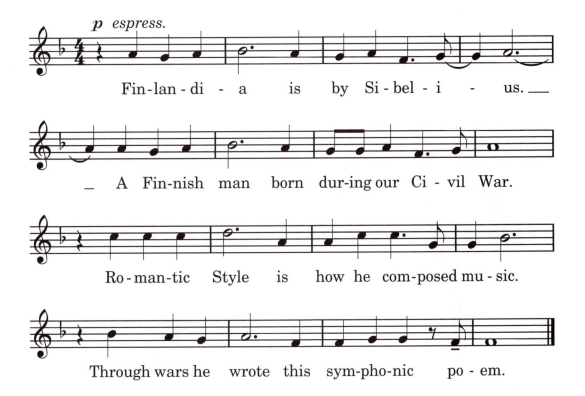

p espress.

Fin-lan-di - a   is   by Si-bel-i - us. ___

_ A Fin-nish man   born dur-ing our Ci - vil War.

Ro-man-tic   Style   is   how he com-posed mu - sic.

Through wars he   wrote this sym-pho-nic   po - em.

Rhythm Card Page

Rhythm Activity Page

Count and clap the following exercises.

1.

1   2   3   and 4
tah tah rest - tee tah

2.

3.

4.

Fill in the missing notes. Use at least one ♪ per measure.

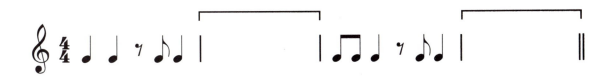

185

Rhapsody in Blue
(GERSHWIN)

Lesson Plan

Objective: Students will identify composers with their country.

Materials: Piano
Copies of the Composers Activity Page
Copies of the Composer Map List and Map of the U.S. and Europe

Procedure: 1. *Tell the story* of *Rhapsody in Blue* to the students.
2. *Teach the tune* to the students.
3. *Focus the lesson* on composers and their nationality.

Activity Page: Have the students (in groups or individually) place each composer into the column they feel is most appropriate: American, European or Russian. Discuss the correct answers.

Activity: Put students into different groups. Ask them to discuss the characteristics of the composers and their tunes and decide what makes each composer uniquely American, European, or Russian. (*Example:* Copland—from New York and wrote about a rodeo.) Regroup the class and discuss what the students found.

Composer Map: The students should draw a line from a composer's country to an open space and write in the composer's name.

Answer Key: Composers Activity Page

  American: Copland, Gershwin, Sousa

  European: Mozart, Beethoven, Bach, Brahms, Schubert, Mendelssohn, Haydn, Rossini, Sibelius, Chopin, Verdi, Bizet

  Russian: Tchaikovsky, Stravinsky, Rachmaninoff

Story of *Rhapsody in Blue*

Rhapsody in Blue was written by George Gershwin, an American composer born in Brooklyn, New York. The Rhapsody was originally written for piano and dance band. Later it was arranged for piano and symphony orchestra. This concerto (music for orchestra and solo or soloists) combines the styles of jazz and classical music. Gershwin was primarily known as a composer of show tunes when, in 1924, he composed the Rhapsody for a band leader. Gershwin finished the music within a month in order to have it performed for a concert in New York. The Rhapsody broke new ground in music, breaking the myth that jazz had limitations.

Gershwin was always seeking to study with as many composers as he would be allowed. In Hollywood, he became a friend and tennis partner of the great composer Arnold Schoenberg. Eventually, he approached his friend about studying composition with him. Schoenberg replied, " I would only make you a bad Schoenberg, and you are such a good Gershwin."

Musical Excerpt
from *Rhapsody in Blue*
GEORGE GERSHWIN (1898–1937)

George Ger-shwin was a com - po-ser you see. From New York _ he wrote Blue Rhap-so - dy. _____ They call it Rhap-so - dy In Blue. Known for his jazz and class-i-cal style: A u -nique nine-teen hun-dreds com-po - ser. _

Composers Activity Page

Place each of the following composers in the correct column on the chart below.

Mozart	Copland	Sousa
Tchaikovsky	Schubert	Rossini
Beethoven	Mendelssohn	Sibelius
Bach	Haydn	Chopin
Brahms	Gershwin	Verdi
Stravinsky	Rachmaninoff	Bizet

American	European	Russian

Composer Map List

Directions: On the map of the U.S. and Europe, draw a line from each composer's country to an open space in the oceans or seas and write in his name.

United States
Copland
Sousa
Gershwin

Russia
Tchaikovsky
Rachmaninoff
Stravinsky
Rimsky-Korsakoff

Finland
Sibelius

Austria
Schubert
Strauss, Johann
Mozart
Haydn

France
Chopin
Bizet
Offenbach
Berlioz

Italy
Verdi
Rossini
Vivaldi

Germany
Schumann
Bach
Mendelssohn
Beethoven
Brahms
Pachelbel
Handel
Strauss, Richard

England
Clarke

Hungary
Liszt

Norway
Grieg

Chechoslavokia
Dvorak

Name _____

Map of the U.S. and Europe

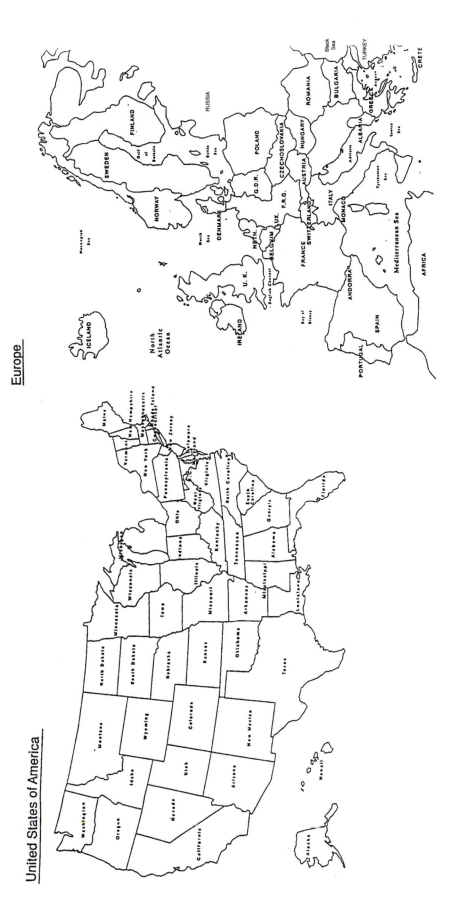

Europe

United States of America

Minuet in G
(BEETHOVEN)

Lesson Plan

Objective: Students will identify and perform a minuet.

Materials: Piano
Copies of the Minuet Activity Page

Procedure:
1. *Tell the story* of the *Minuet in G* to the students.
2. *Teach the tune* to the students.
3. *Focus the lesson* on the minuet. Ask the students how many beats are in a measure for the minuet (3). The words to the tune will remind them. Review Bach's *Little Minuet in G*.
4. *Activity:* Using Bach's *Little Minuet in G* or a recording of the entire piece, have the students tap their legs on beat one and clap their hands on beats two and three for the first section of the piece. If you use a recording or you play the second section of the piece, have the students stomp on one and snap fingers on beats two and three. Try other minuets with the same activity.

Activity Page: Have the students circle the measure that would best fit in a minuet. The second part is for the student to create his/her minuet through writing the rhythms. Possibly, have each student clap their minuet.

Level IV Quiz: Give students copies of the quiz on page 197. Using the Composer/Tune/Country Bank, have them fill in the correct responses to the order of tunes you play.

Story of *Minuet in G*

The minuet is a dance in triple meter (i.e., 3/4 or 3/8 timing). It was originated about 100 years before Beethoven, but he made some changes in it, even changing it to a scherzo.

Some people say that Beethoven was a cranky old man, but perhaps his mind, many times, was somewhere else. A story that reminds us of how Beethoven didn't always realize what was going on tells us a little bit about him and his personality. One evening, Beethoven attended a dinner party at a count's house. He was asked to improvise (make up music off the top of his head) on the piano but he refused. Soon afterwards, the guests were summoned to the table, in the dining room. As they started their meal, they began to hear more and more sounds coming from the next room where the piano was placed. Guest by guest, one by one, they each left the table and moved over to the room in which Beethoven was playing. Finally, all the guests were standing around him. Then suddenly, Beethoven remembered being called to the table for dinner, and he jumped up and ran so quickly that he fell over a table full of china. The count chuckled and all the guests slowly walked back to the table to finish dinner; or, in Beethoven's case, to start to eat dinner.

Musical Excerpt from *Minuet in G*
LUDWIG VAN BEETHOVEN
(1770–1827)

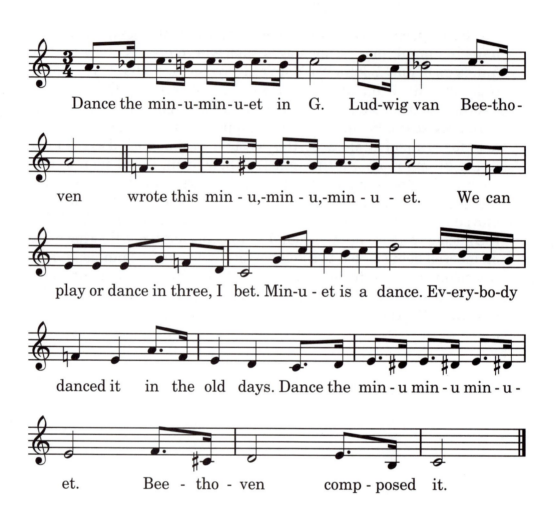

Little Minuet in G
J. S. BACH

Minuet Activity Page

Circle the measure that could possibly be part of a minuet.

Write your own rhythmical minuet.

MINUET

by _____

Classic Tunes Level IV Quiz

Use the composer bank below to help you name the tune you hear.

	TUNE	*COMPOSER*	*COUNTRY*
1.			
2.			
3.			
4.			
5.			

COMPOSER/TUNE/COUNTRY BANK

Bach	*Emperor's String Quartet*	Germany
Haydn	*Minuet in G*	Austria
Sibelius	*Fugue*	U.S.A.
Gershwin	*Finlandia*	Germany
Beethoven	*Rhapsody in Blue*	Finland

The Barber of Seville
(ROSSINI)

Lesson Plan

Objective: Students will identify and define significant terms and parts of an opera.

Materials: Piano
Copies of the Opera Terms Page
Cards made from the Opera Term Cards Page
Various props
Copies of the Opera Terms Activity Page

Procedure:
1. ***Tell the story*** of *The Barber of Seville* to the students.
2. ***Teach the tune*** to the students.
3. ***Focus the lesson*** on opera. Use the Opera Terms to help define the following terms:

Aria	Comic Opera
Chorus	Grand Opera
Finale	Serious Opera
Libretto	Tragic Opera
Overture	
Recitative	

4. ***Review*** all opera tunes and tales learned thus far.
5. ***Activity:*** Make enough copies of the Opera Term Cards for each student. Using the aria, recitative, chorus, libretto, overture, and finale cards, describe the opera terms for each opera through the use of narratives and props. Ask the students to "Decide how each of these terms is used in each of the operas. Keep in mind the tunes and tales you've learned so far."
6. ***Activity:*** Group the students in teams of three or four. Write the opera tunes and titles of *Don Giovanni, The Barber of Seville, William Tell, Rigoletto*, and *Carmen* on the board. Have the teams decide which type of opera the tunes and tales describe best. Regroup the class as a whole, and by using the term cards for the types of operas, have the students raise the card that best fits the tune and tale of each learned opera.

Activity Page: Have the students read and fill in the blanks of the story with the correct term.

Answer Key: Opera Terms Activity Page
Opera . . . Verdi . . . Rossini . . . Bizet . . . Mozart . . . Grand . . . Comic . . . Tragic . . . Overture . . . Libretto . . . Recitative . . . Aria . . . Chorus . . . Finale.

Story of *The Barber of Seville*

This story is about a count who is in love with Rosina, who is the ward of a doctor. The doctor is Rosina's guardian, but he also intends to be her husband. While the doctor is planning his strategy to marry Rosina, Figaro, the town barber, jack-of-all-trades and busybody, finds out about the count's love for Rosina. He decides to try to help the count win her heart. However, the count wants Rosina to love him for himself, not because he is the count. So, the count, on Figaro's advice, uses several disguises to help win Rosina's true heart. The count gets in to see Rosina a few times and sends many love notes to her. So, Rosina falls in love with him. Now, Figaro must devise plans so the two lovers can get together and elope. One includes disguising the count as a military guard who does not know what he is doing. Rosina, not knowing the guard is her lover, asks Figaro, who is there to give the doctor a shave, to deliver the note to the count. However, the doctor notices she is trying to pass a note. The doctor, with the shaving cream on his face and the apron around his neck, goes running around the room trying to grab this note which is being passed back and forth by Figaro, the guard, and Rosina. But the count grabs it and sees it's a laundry list, cleverly substituted by Rosina. The doctor has the guard arrested, but they soon release him. Figaro has a final plan. He disguises the count as Rosina's music teacher's assistant, who comes to the doctor's house to give Rosina her music lesson. The doctor is suspicious, however he dozes off during the lesson. He wakes up, realizes what is going on, and goes after the police and notary to do the marriage ceremony for him and Rosina. Figaro tries to help the young lovers escape, but fails. When the doctor returns with the notary, Figaro pushes the count and Rosina up to the notary who marries them on the spot. The count tells her his real identity, and the couple lives happily ever after. And the doctor is happy because he finds that he can keep Rosina's dowry without marrying Rosina.

Musical Excerpt
from *The Barber of Seville*
GIOACCHINO ROSSINI (1792–1868)

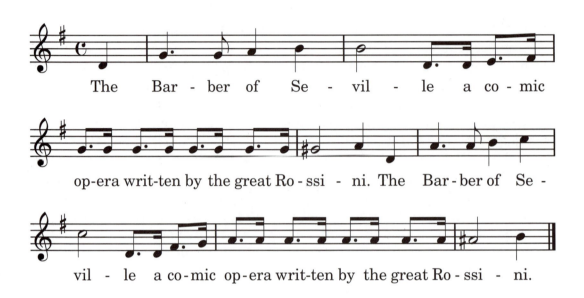

200

Opera Terms Page

PARTS OF AN OPERA

Aria—an opera song.

Chorus—music in which the secondary cast or large group sings.

Finale—the ending music or ending section of an opera.

Libretto—the script of an opera.

Overture—the opening or beginning of an opera. It contains musical excerpts of the entire opera.

Recitative—the sung dialog of an opera.

TYPES OF OPERAS

Comic—opera with a comic or funny subject.

Grand—opera done as a grand, extravagant production.

Serious—opera with a serious subject.

Tragic—a subject with tragedy.

ARIA

CHORUS

RECITATIVE

FINALE

LIBRETTO

OVERTURE

SERIOUS OPERA

COMIC OPERA

GRAND OPERA

TRAGIC OPERA

Opera Terms Activity Page

In the following discussion of opera, fill in each blank with the correct word from the word bank below.

OPERA

An _____ is a play that is completely performed with music. Some of the great opera composers were the Italians _____ and _____, the Frenchman _____ and the Austrian composer _____ who composed *Don Giovanni*.

There are different types of operas. The _____ opera is big and lavishly done. A funny and light-hearted opera is called a _____ opera. And of course, in the _____ opera someone usually comes to their demise.

Opera is made up of many parts and sections. The opening music before the opera starts is called the _____. The _____ is the script of the opera. _____ is the sung dialog, but the lyrical song is an _____. When the entire cast sings it is called the _____. Finally, the opera ending is called the _____.

Opera Word Bank

Recitative	Grand	Verdi
Opera	Serious	Rossini
Aria	Comic	Mozart
Overture	Tragic	Bizet
Chorus		
Libretto		
Finale		

Wedding Chorus
(WAGNER)

Lesson Plan

Objective: Students will identify and perform the rhythm ♪. ♪.

Materials: Piano
Rhythm Card Page
Copies of the Musical Excerpt from *Wedding Chorus*
Copies of the Rhythm Activity Page
Drums or rhythm sticks

Procedure: 1. ***Tell the story*** of *Wedding Chorus* to the students.

2. ***Teach the tune*** to the students.

3   ***Echo clap*** the following rhythms. Perhaps, use sticks.

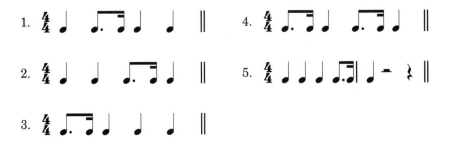

4. ***Name and display*** the rhythm to the students, using the Rhythm Card. Have the students count the dotted-sixteenth as tee-ka or 1- da. Show the break down of the subdivision ♫♫ = ti-ka-ti-ka or 1e+a.

5. ***Play*** examples of familiar songs with the ♪. ♪ rhythm. Try: "Battle Hymn of the Republic" and *Barber of Seville*.

6. **Activity:** Give each student a copy of the tune. Have students circle each ♪. ♪ rhythm. Play the tune, ask them to raise their hand when they hear each ♪. ♪ —they may use a copy of the tune to help. Finally, have the students sing and clap the rhythm of the entire tune.

Activity Page: Clap the rhythms on the activity page (teacher's edition) for the students. Have them circle the beat number for which the ♪. ♪ rhythm occurs. The second part is for dictation. The students will write the rhythms you play or clap.

Story of *Wedding Chorus*

The first production of *Lohengrin* was given by Franz Liszt, Wagner's father-in-law.

The opera story takes place in Germany during the 10th century. The king has come to the city to collect an army to fight the invading Hungarians. He finds that the succession to the dukedom is being disputed by Frederick and Elsa, the daughter of the late duke. Elsa's brother, the rightful heir, has mysteriously disappeared, and Elsa is accused of murdering him. The king orders that a fight take place to determine the rightful heir. No knight wants to fight for Elsa. So she prays that a dream she has had of a knight protector may come true. To everyone's astonishment, trumpets herald as a swan-drawn boat sails down the river with Lohengrin, her knight protector. Lohengrin and Elsa plan to marry if he is victorious. However, no one knows Lohengrin's name, and Elsa promises never to ask him what it is.

Lohengrin defeats Frederick. Although Frederick and his wife are banished from the city, they try to get revenge on Elsa. At the wedding, Elsa is about to start down the aisle when the two plotters try to convince Elsa that Lohengrin is evil. Unfortunately, Elsa forgets herself and asks Lohengrin his name. He tells her he must leave because she has broken her promise. The swan-drawn boat arrives to pick Lohengrin up. The swan turns out to be Elsa's brother, the rightful heir to the dukedom, and everyone realizes that Lohengrin is the Knight of the Holy Grail. Now the boat is drawn by a dove and carries off Lohengrin.

Musical Excerpt
from the *Wedding Chorus (Lohengrin)*
RICHARD WAGNER (1813–1883)

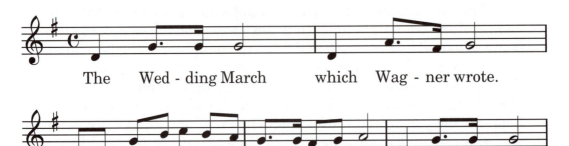

The   Wed - ding March   which   Wag - ner wrote.

Lo-hen-grin the o-pera is where it came from. The Wed-ding March

which Wag-ner wrote.   It's played for wed-dings   much of to-day.

Name _____

Rhythm Activity Page
(Teacher's Edition)

Clap the following rhythms for the students. They will circle the beat(s) in which the rhythm occurs.

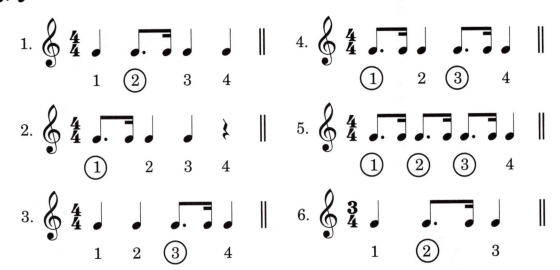

Have the students write in the beats of the following rhythms as you clap or play on a drum.

Rhythm Activity Page

Circle the number of the beat(s) in which you hear the ♩. ♪ rhythm.

1. 𝄞 4/4   1   2   3   4   ‖   4. 𝄞 4/4   1   2   3   4   ‖

2. 𝄞 4/4   1   2   3   4   ‖   5. 𝄞 4/4   1   2   3   4   ‖

3. 𝄞 4/4   1   2   3   4   ‖   6. 𝄞 3/4   1   2   3   ‖

Write in the correct notation of the following rhythms you hear. You will only need to use ♩. ♪ and ♩ 's.

1. 𝄞 4/4   ‖   3. 𝄞 4/4   ‖

2. 𝄞 4/4   ‖   4. 𝄞 3/4   ‖

Il Trovatore
(Verdi)

Lesson Plan

Objective: The students will identify the different voice terms of soprano, alto, tenor, baritone, bass, mezzo, cambiata, and a capella.

Materials: Piano
Copies of the Voice Terms Activity Page
Copies of the Voice Page
Blank construction paper
Dark crayons or markers

Procedure: 1. ***Tell the story*** of *Il Trovatore* to the students.

2. ***Teach the tune*** to the students. Ask the question: "Does *Il Trovatore's* Anvil Chorus have the rhythm of ♪. ♪ ?"

3. ***Define*** the term andante as a leisurely walking tempo (slow).

4. ***Focus the lesson*** on voice ranges and terms. Use the Voice Page.

5. ***Activity:*** Group the students into teams of three to five. Select one student from each team, and give him or her a copy of the Voice Page. Have students take turns reading the term and definition of each voice until all the terms have been read. Ask the students to make a Term Card for each voice, and display each card in the middle of them sitting in a circle. Have one student read the definition of a term (randomly) and the rest of the team decide what term it is and turn over its card if they are correct. Have the students rotate the Voice Page around the circle, so each has a chance to read and name the term.

Activity Page: Have the students fill in the low to high mountain spaces with the names for the low to high voices of men and women.

Answer Key: Voice Terms Activity Page
Women (Low to High): Contralto, Alto, Mezzo-Soprano, Soprano.
Men (Low to High): Bass, Baritone, Tenor, Falsetto.

Story of *Il Trovatore* (Anvil Chorus)

The Anvil Chorus from *Il Trovatore* was written by the great Italian opera composer Giuseppe Verdi (1813–1901).

In 1899, Verdi was aware that his friend Leopoldo was making many trips to an opera house to supervise the playing of bells for the opera *Tosca*.

Verdi asked, "How many bells are being used and what are they used for?" The conductor said, "Eleven, and they are used in the third act to represent dawn breaking over Rome with the chimes of the different churches."

"Eleven bells!" exclaimed Verdi. And to think that when I composed *Il Trovatore* I was afraid to introduce one bell for the fear the impresarios would be upset. There's nothing more to say except that the world has progressed—the operatic world, at least.

Il Trovatore is a Spanish tragedy about people's terrible pasts, love, and revenge. The Anvil Chorus is the most recognized music of the entire opera.

Musical Excerpt from *Il Trovatore*
(Anvil Chorus)
GIUSEPPE VERDI (1813–1901)

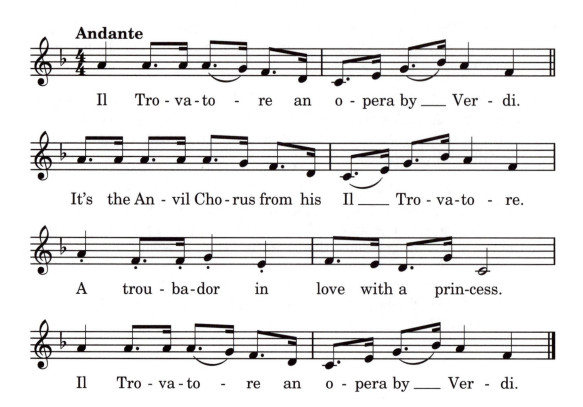

Il Tro - va - to - re an o - pera by Ver - di.

It's the An - vil Cho - rus from his Il Tro - va - to - re.

A trou - ba - dor in love with a prin - cess.

Il Tro - va - to - re an o - pera by Ver - di.

© 1997 by Parker Publishing Company

Voice Page
Voices and Terms

Soprano: The highest of the voice range. Women and elementary students sing at this range.

Mezzo-soprano: The next highest voice. Mezzo means half or medium. Again, women and children usually sing in this range.

Alto: The lower woman's voice, but isn't as low as the contralto.

Tenor: The highest of the male voices. Boys do not sing in this range until their voice changes.

Baritone: The middle voice of the male.

Bass: The lowest of all voices.

Cambiata voice: The range boys can sing when their voice is changing. This usually occurs during the middle school or high school years.

A capella: The term used for singing without instrumental accompaniment.

Falsetto: The voice men can use which is higher than their natural voice.

Name _____

Voice Terms Activity Page

Place the voice that relates to the highness or lowness in the range of men and women.

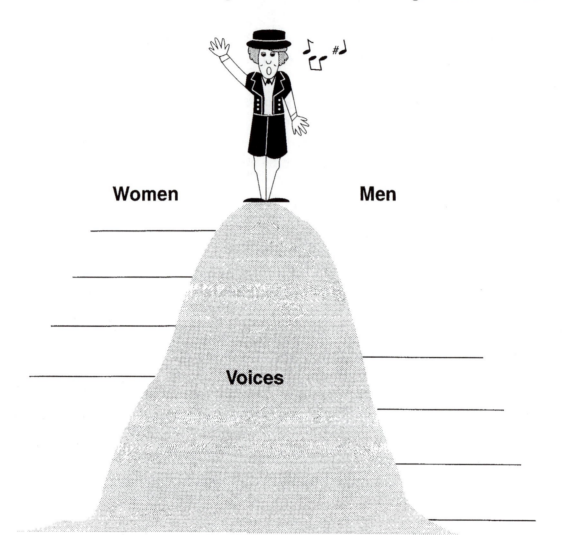

Alto	Baritone
Bass	Mezzo-soprano
Tenor	Soprano
Contralto	Falsetto

© 1997 by Parker Publishing Company

Aida
(VERDI)

Lesson Plan

Objective: Students will identify and perform the triplet rhythm ♪♪♪ .

Materials: Piano
Triplet Rhythm Card Page
Copies of the Triplet Rhythm Activity Page

Procedure: 1. ***Tell the story*** of *Aida* to the students.

2. ***Teach the tune*** to the students.

3. ***Focus the lesson*** on the triplet. Name the rhythm and teach the students how to count it. "One-Trip-let," "tri-p-let," cho-co-late, straw-ber-ry, etc. Choose the one that best fits your program. Use the Rhythm Card to assist you.

4. ***Echo clap*** (or use rhythm instruments) the following rhythms:

5. ***Activity:*** Using the following measures of rhythms, have the students complete the incomplete measures with each of the student responses. The teacher is to clap the given measures.

Student Responses:

Rhythm Measures:

Note: Use one student response at a time for all incomplete rhythm measures.

Activity Page: Have the students create their own compositions. Be sure they can clap the given exercise. Perhaps, try the whole class performing each student's composition(s).

Story of *Aida*

Aida takes place in ancient Africa in the times of the pharaohs. A man chosen to be the leader of the Egyptian army is longing to impress a slave girl, Aida. However, the general is loved by the daughter of the Egyptian King. And the king's daughter realizes the general's love for Aida, who is the daughter of the enemy's king. Both Aida and the general are torn between love and their patriotism for their countries. The general goes off to war, and he is victorious. Upon his return home, the king asks the general to marry his daughter. The general refuses and tries to get the enemy war prisoners released, but is unsuccessful. For his actions he is condemned to prison in a sealed crypt. When the stone has been sealed, he discovers that Aida is waiting there for him. And the two lovers live the remainder of their lives together.

Aida is a grand opera written by the famous Italian opera composer Giuseppe Verdi.

Verdi was quite a national figure in his day. He was revered by many fans and musicians. Once, a cello player, who joined Verdi's orchestra at La Scala for the first time, was so overwhelmed by Verdi's great music he returned to his home that night and awakened his mother from sleep to have her join him on his knees saying: " Viva, Verdi!" The bewildered woman complied.

Musical Excerpt from *Aida*
(Triumphal March)
FORTUNIO GIUSEPPE VERDI
(1813–1901)

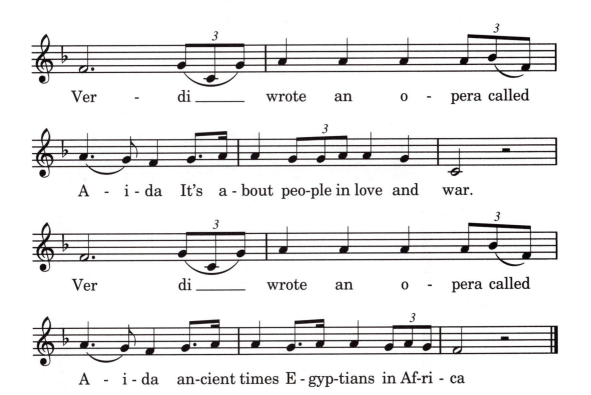

Ver - di ___ wrote an o - pera called

A - i - da It's a - bout peo-ple in love and war.

Ver - di ___ wrote an o - pera called

A - i - da an-cient times E - gyp-tians in Af-ri - ca

Triplet Rhythm Card Page

© 1997 by Parker Publishing Company

Triplet Rhythm Activity Page

Count and clap the examples of triplets below.

TRIPLET

1   2   3   4

Compose your own triplet exercises.

Symphony No 40
(MOZART)

Lesson Plan

Objective: Students will recognize and identify the dotted note concept.

Materials: Piano
Copy of Dotted-Note Page and Dotted-Note Rhythm Card
Copies of the Dotted-Note Activity Page
Copies of the Opera Wordsearch

Procedure:
1. **Tell the story** of *Symphony No. 40* to the students.
2. **Teach the tune** to the students. Ask the students if it is major or minor, fast or slow, and what tempo would best fit this tune. The tempo is allegretto—fast, but not as fast as allegro. However, it is faster than moderato.
3. **Focus the lesson** on the dotted-note. Use the Dotted-Note Page and Dotted-Note Rhythm Card to help you explain it.
4. **Activity:** In a round-robin technique and while using the Dotted-Note Page, show each student a dotted-note, and have them tell you how many beats it receives. It can be monotonous, but quite effective.
5. **Activity:** Use the dotted-note cards as a deck of cards. Fan the cards out in your hand. Be sure the note cannot be seen. Have the students pick a card and tell you either the amount of beats it receives or what it is called. You could also have the student explain how they arrived at the answer. Perhaps try the students in teams and competing.

Activity Page: The student must write in the correct amount of beats for the dotted-notes representing the depth levels getting to the bottom of the sea where the sunken treasure lies.

Additional Activity Page: Students will enjoy completing the Opera Wordsearch at the end of this lesson.

Answer Key: Dotted-Note Activity Page
Level 1 = 3 beats, Level 2 = 6 beats, Level 3 = 1 1/2 beats, Level 4 = 3/4 beats.

Story of *Symphony No. 40*

The 1780s were a time of maturity for the classical symphony. That was when Mozart composed his last three symphonies: 39, 40, and 41. Number 40 was in G Minor, which Mozart often used as a key for the tragic. No. 40 was also known for not including clarinets, trumpets, or timpani in the orchestration.

During this time of Mozart's career his life really was quite tragic. He earned a modest income as the court composer for the Emperor Joseph II. However, his salary was not enough to keep up with his lavish lifestyle, gambling and partying. He continued to compose in order to supplement his salary. Overworking, drinking, and late hours began to wear Mozart out. Exhausted and plagued by fainting attacks, he developed an overwhelming illness. His hands and feet became swollen and he had a severe fever from which he succumbed at the age of 35. Mozart was given a pauper's funeral, because he died penniless.

Musical Excerpt
from *Symphony No. 40*
W.A. MOZART (1756–1791)

You can sing it you can play it do it Moz-art Sym-pho-

ny For - ty, For - ty. You can sing it you can play it do it

Moz - art Sym-pho - ny For - ty, For - ty.

Dotted-Note Page

A dot found beside a note equals half of the time that the note is worth. For example:

$\textbf{\textit{d}}$ = 2 counts + · ($\frac{1}{2}$ of $\textbf{\textit{d}}$) 1 count.
    equals $\textbf{\textit{d}}$. (3 counts)

$\textbf{\textit{♩}}$ = 1 count + · ($\frac{1}{2}$ of $\textbf{\textit{♩}}$) $\frac{1}{2}$ count.
    equals $\textbf{\textit{♩}}$. (1 and $\frac{1}{2}$ counts)

$\textbf{\textit{♪}}$ = $\frac{1}{2}$ count + · ($\frac{1}{2}$ of $\textbf{\textit{♪}}$) $\frac{1}{4}$ count.
    equals $\textbf{\textit{♪}}$. ($\frac{3}{4}$ counts)

Try to figure out the one below. How many beats (or counts) is it worth?

o.

o + · = ___

Dotted-Note Rhythm Card Page

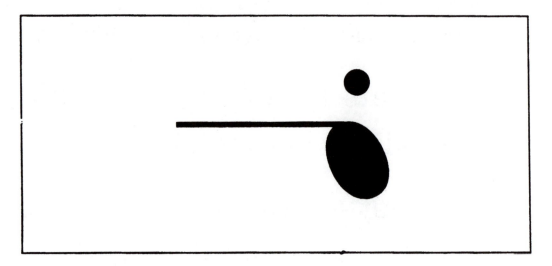

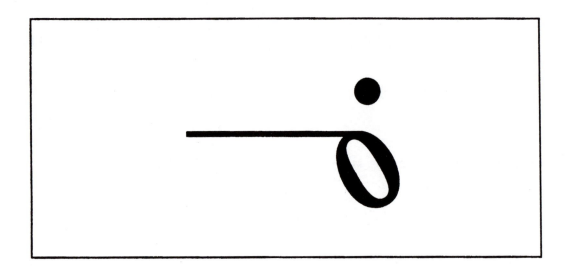

© 1997 by Parker Publishing Company

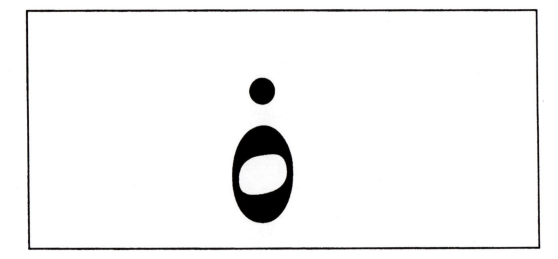

Dotted-Note Activity Page

Directions: Fill in the correct number of beats for each level. If you can reach Level 4, you've found the treasure.

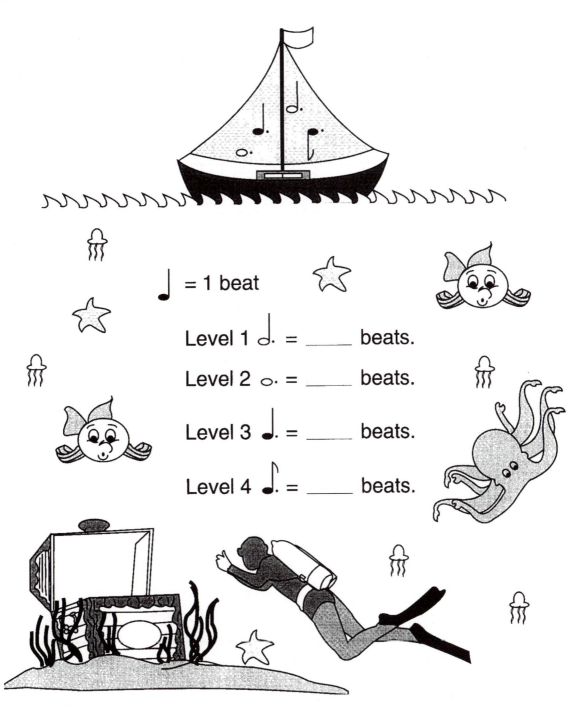

♩ = 1 beat

Level 1 ♩. = _____ beats.

Level 2 o. = _____ beats.

Level 3 ♩. = _____ beats.

Level 4 ♪. = _____ beats.

Opera Wordsearch

W	S	Y	V	P	A	G	F	U	R	Q	Q	A	T	G	J	G	U	A	O
I	E	R	K	C	E	O	I	P	Q	F	K	M	R	M	C	N	L	T	P
Y	R	B	I	U	M	M	G	X	U	G	S	B	A	D	F	K	T	Y	R
P	I	T	I	G	S	E	A	M	X	K	K	L	G	X	V	E	Q	G	E
F	O	F	W	Z	O	X	R	D	R	V	N	Y	I	B	R	H	X	Z	V
R	U	Y	Q	K	E	L	O	O	O	Y	S	K	C	B	D	R	Z	E	I
Z	S	E	A	J	D	T	E	K	I	N	Z	A	I	A	E	X	M	D	T
E	D	N	R	G	K	J	A	T	K	K	G	L	V	H	E	D	W	B	A
R	C	T	I	W	L	I	I	X	T	O	U	I	O	R	J	R	W	A	T
G	V	S	A	U	V	K	D	J	D	O	Y	G	O	C	D	A	E	L	I
E	R	W	L	W	F	C	A	P	D	B	M	A	P	V	F	Y	W	T	C
L	S	A	N	X	A	M	L	H	J	O	U	W	S	X	A	O	W	W	E
R	O	D	N	V	J	G	Y	E	Q	M	O	Z	A	R	T	N	H	O	R
A	L	S	U	D	T	O	N	V	H	O	P	X	R	A	N	B	N	W	L
O	V	E	R	T	U	R	E	E	E	A	V	F	A	O	I	P	T	I	B
B	C	U	T	H	P	C	V	A	R	F	X	L	N	B	S	E	P	Z	V
H	Z	J	Y	T	Q	O	E	M	B	U	F	F	A	M	U	S	A	F	A
D	H	C	E	I	Y	M	R	S	F	I	N	A	L	E	H	Q	I	K	Q
G	G	R	R	S	G	I	D	H	X	J	M	N	R	U	L	D	V	N	X
C	H	O	R	U	S	C	I	O	I	F	X	G	W	U	Z	J	Y	Y	I

1. ARIA
2. CHORUS
3. RECITATIVE
4. LIBRETTO
5. OVERTURE
6. FINALE
7. SERIOUS
8. TRAGIC
9. COMIC
10. GRAND
11. BUFFA
12. MOZART
13. BIZET
14. VERDI
15. ROSSINI
16. WAGNER
17. RIGOLETTO
18. FIGARO
19. AIDA
20. DONGIOVANNI

Name _____

Opera Wordsearch
Answer Key

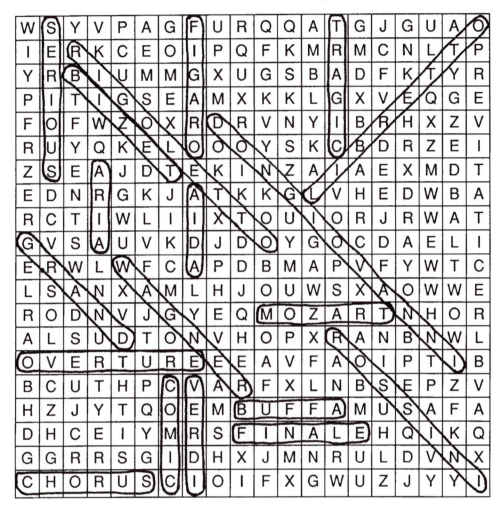

1. ARIA
2. CHORUS
3. RECITATIVE
4. LIBRETTO
5. OVERTURE
6. FINALE
7. SERIOUS
8. TRAGIC
9. COMIC
10. GRAND
11. BUFFA
12. MOZART
13. BIZET
14. VERDI
15. ROSSINI
16. WAGNER
17. RIGOLETTO
18. FIGARO
19. AIDA
20. DONGIOVANNI

227

Classic Tunes Level IV Test
Teacher's Edition

Listening

Play the following tunes in the given order:

Title
1. *Wedding March*
2. *Aida*
3. *Barber of Seville*
4. *Il Trovatore*
5. *Symphony No. 40*

Terms

Define the following terms.
1. Aria—an opera song
2. Libretto—the script of an opera
3. Overture—the opening or beginning section of an opera
4. Recitative—dialog or conversation which is sung in an opera
5. Soprano—the highest voice, usually sung by women or children

Rhythm

Circle the incorrect measure for each line of music.

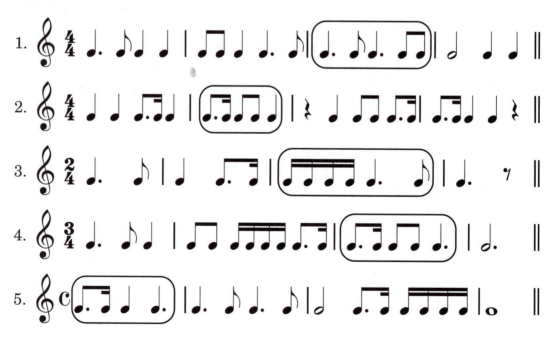

Classic Tunes Level IV Test

Listening

Name the title of each of the following tunes you hear.

Title

1. _____

2. _____

3. _____

4. _____

5. _____

Terms

Define the following terms:

1. Aria:_____

2. Libretto: _____

3. Overture: _____

4. Recitative: _____

5. Soprano: _____

Rhythm

Circle the incorrect measure for each line of music.

1.

2.

3.

4.

5.

LEVEL V:
(GRADE LEVELS: 5-8)

La Gioconda
(PONCIELLI)

Lesson Plan

Objective: Students will identify the pick-up (anacrusis) note.

Materials: Piano
                    Copies of the Musical Excerpt from *La Gioconda*
                    Chalkboard
                    Note Value Cards
                    Copies of the Pick-Up Note Activity Page

Procedure: 1. *Tell the story* of La Gioconda to the students.

                    2. *Teach the tune* to the students.

                    3. *Focus the lesson* on the pick-up note. Point out that the be-
                       ginning notes are in an incomplete measure. Give students the
                       chance to realize the last measure is incomplete, too. "What is
                       the relationship between the two measures?" Lead the students
                       through the process of learning that when the two measures are
                       added together they equal the amount of beats for one measure.
                       Use the activity page to help students understand the pick-up
                       note with more assurance.

                    4. *Activity:* Use several note cards of any variety of note values.
                       Place magnetic tape on the back of the cards, or tape, if not
                       using a magnetic board. Use your chalkboard to place a few
                       complete measures of rhythms. Save the first and last measures
                       for students to build their own pick-ups.

                    5. *Activity:* Play a variety of tunes. Ask the students to raise their
                       hands if the tune contains one or more pick-up notes. The fol-
                       lowing tunes are possible examples: *Adagio* (with a pickup),
                       Stars and Stripes (with), *La Gioconda* (with), *Happy Farmer*
                       (with), *Don Giovanni* (without), *Eine Kleine Nacht Musik* (with-
                       out), *Hallelujah Chorus* (without), and *Rigoletto* (without). Be
                       sure that students understand that pick-up notes are not on the
                       strongest beat of the measure.

Activity Page: The first part calls on students to fill in the correct meter/time sig-
                    nature. The second part requires students to create their own pick-
                    up notes.

Story of *La Gioconda*
(Dance of the Hours)

Barnaba, a storyteller, has for some time fancied a singer named Gioconda. However, Gioconda has a crush on Enzo, a sailor. To Gionconda's dismay, Enzo is in love with Laura, the betrothed of the influential head of the Spanish Inquisition, Alvise.

Being jealous of Enzo's fortune to be fancied by Gioconda, Barnaba decides to spread rumors about Enzo and Laura. Alvise hears of these rumors and decides to avenge Enzo and Laura. Gioconda decides to protect Laura by giving her a drug to put her into a deep sleep. Alvise thinks she is dead, and he puts Enzo in prison. Although Enzo fancies Laura, she decides to help get Enzo released from prison by giving her reluctant love to Barnaba, because he can talk to Alvise to have him released.

Enzo is released from prison. Laura and Enzo run off together, and Barnaba and Gioconda remain behind.

Musical Excerpt from *La Gioconda* (Dance of the Hours)
AMILCARE PONCHIELLI (1834–1886)

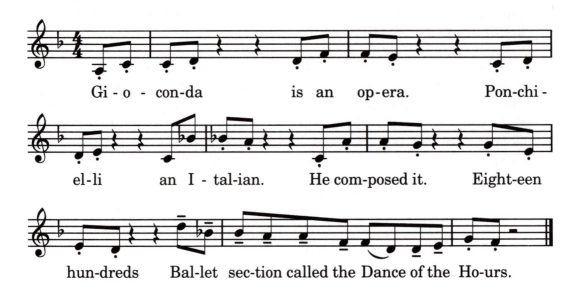

Gi - o - con-da   is an   op-era.   Pon-chi -

el-li   an I - tal-ian.   He com-posed it.   Eight-een

hun-dreds   Bal-let   sec-tion called the Dance of the Ho-urs.

234

Pick-Up Note Activity Page

The Pick-Up Note

EXAMPLE:

Fill in the correct meter of these lines.

Write out your own pick-up notes to the following lines.

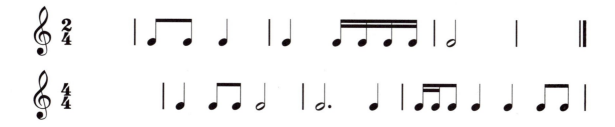

235

Liebestraum
(LISZT)

Lesson Plan

Objective: Students will identify and define the terms for music forms: nocturne, serenade, rondo, fugue, theme and variations, and suite.

Materials: Piano
Copies of the Musical Excerpt from *Liebestraum*
Copies of the Music Forms Activity Page
Copies of the 6 Form Pages

Procedure:
1. **Tell the story** of *Liebestraum* to the students.
2. **Teach the tune** to the students.
3. **Focus the lesson** on form. Use the Form Pages to help define the terms. The Form Shapes may be used for more in-depth lesson(s). Use this activity to help you teach students the given forms through movement or acting.

    • Make a moon shape with your arms to symbolize a nocturne.

    • For the serenade, hold a guitar or an invisible one and serenade the class.

    • For the rondo, take five or seven students to do different motions. Have them form a straight line. The first, third and fifth (and seventh) students do jumping jacks. The second student can jog, and the fourth student can do knee bends (sixth student can stand still).

    • To display a fugue, select four students and have them walk around the room. Be sure each one starts at a different time. Once they all have started, they should walk together in different ways, such as jumping, jogging, hopping, walking and then separate again or end together.

    • To explain theme and variations, have a few students stand up in front of the class. Point out differences in hair color, height, and clothes' colors.

    • For the suite, choose five or six students to do the following: dance in ballroom style, dance the twist, dance the swim, dance an improvised style, and any other popular or known dance to depict a suite of dances.

    Another possible way to describe a suite is to have the students act out eating in a kitchen, sleeping in a bedroom, washing in a bathroom, watching television in the living room, etc.

4. **Activity:** Put the students into five or six groups. Assign each group a term: suite, theme and variations, fugue, rondo, and nocturne , of the particular Form Page, to assist them in learning what their form is and how it works. As they discover how their form works, have them decide on how to explain and teach the other groups. This activity can be time-consuming; nevertheless, it will be constructive. Allow students to use their creativity. Additionally, it is very beneficial to use listening examples of each form.

Activity Page: Students will draw a line to the graphic that best corresponds with the form.

Story of *Liebestraum*

Liebestraum, which means "Love's Dream," was written by a very handsome, romantic man who had many loves; always a new girlfriend. He was also a very talented pianist, maybe the greatest. This man was Franz Liszt. Liszt was the Hungarian-born composer who wrote *Liebestraum* around 1847 as a song, then eventually changed it into a piano piece. Even though he composed three *Liebestraums*, this particular nocturne (night song) is the most recognized.

Liszt was quite popular with the Russians, so, frequently, he was invited to the Russian palace of Czar Nicholas to perform recitals. The Czar was not known for being an avid music lover, however it was a sign of power and influence to be able to have performers such as Liszt at your beck and call. During one of the recitals, the Czar was talking very loudly to a lady sitting near him. Liszt, perturbed, stopped playing. The Czar asked Liszt, "Why did you stop?" Liszt condescendingly responded: "When the emperor speaks, the people should listen."

Musical Excerpt from *Liebestraum*
FRANZ LISZT (1811–1886)

Franz Liszt, he wrote a piece __ of mu - sic for pi -
an - o; he called it Lie - bes - traum. __
Hun - ga - ri - an he was __ He wrote this pi - an - o
D.C. al Fine
tune __ a noc - turne . . . Night - time tune. __

Form Page

Nocturne

The nocturne is an 1800–1900's instrumental piece; usually written for the piano. The word nocturne is French for "of the night." Debussy and Chopin were composers of the nocturne, however, *Liebestraum* (Love's Dream) is a famous nocturne by Franz Liszt.

Form Page

Serenade

The serenade is a vocal or instrumental work intended for performance in the evening and usually for a friend, love, or important person. The custom of serenading began during the Renaissance Period (1400–1600), when an admirer would stand below a balcony or window and sing. During the 1700–1800s a more serious serenade was written for special occasions. Mozart, Beethoven, Dvorak, and Tchaikovsky were some of the most famous of the serenade composers. The classical form is usually in three sections (movements): fast-slow-fast.

Form Page

Rondo

A rondo is a music form with many sections; however, a main theme or section recurs. The recurring section or theme acts as a refrain. When referring to music form, letters are often assigned to sections (i.e., A, B, C, E, E, etc.) The typical rondo is usually designed as an ABACA form, the A section being the recurring theme. Other combinations like ABACADA, ABACABA, and ABACBA have been used. The rondo form originated during the Baroque Period, but was quite popular during the Classical Period. Aside from using letters, geometric shapes are also ideal for understanding form. Below is an example of a rondo form using shapes.

Form Page

Fugue

Fugue is French for "flight." It is of imitative form as the round or canon. The theme is stated in all the voices successively with a polyphonic (multi-sounds and melodies woven together) texture. The fugue can employ two to six voices; usually three or four. The subject (main theme) is presented, then followed by the answer (imitation) in the second voice. The third voice then appears with the subject and the fourth voice with its imitation or answer. The music develops until the subject and answer reappear.

The following diagram gives an abbreviated visual concept of a fugue.

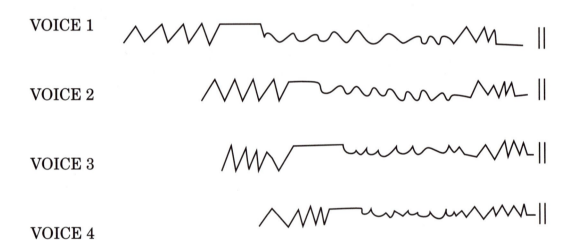

* It is similar to a constant hand-off lateral play in football!

Form Page

Theme and Variations

A theme and variations form is one of the most basic concepts. A theme is usually presented, followed by music that is a modification of the theme. The theme and variations are individual pieces which share a commonality, but differ in some musical fashion. The variations could differ from the theme by rhythm, meter, mode, texture, tempo, instrumentation, or dynamics. The graphic below may give you a better picture of the theme and variations form.

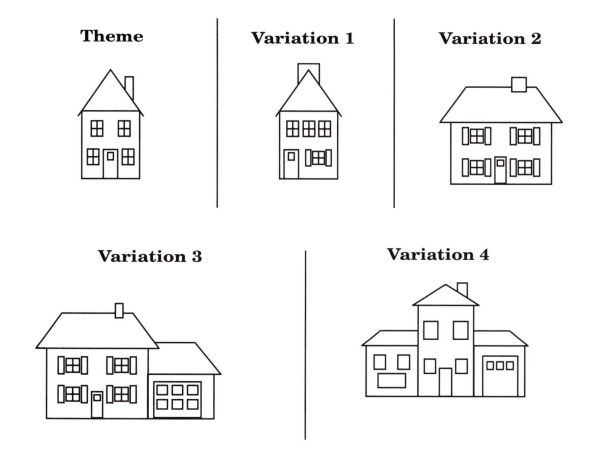

Theme

Variation 1

Variation 2

Variation 3

Variation 4

Form Page

Suite

A suite (French for "succession" or "following") is instrumental music with a series of movements with something in common. The suite began during the Renaissance Period, but flourished during the Baroque Period. The Baroque solo suite was made up of dances with different rhythms and speeds. Handel and Bach were two famous composers of suites.

When trying to learn about the suite, it is helpful to think of the hotel suite. The hotel suite is a group or series of rooms which a person rents per day. Use the diagram below to help you understand the suite.

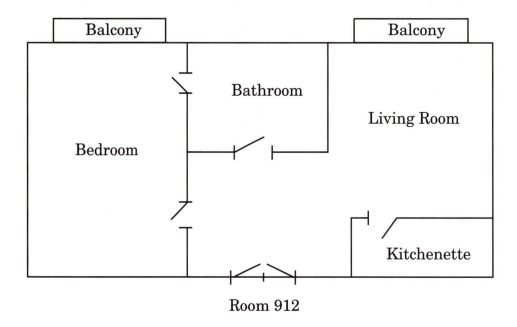

Room 912

Form Shape Page

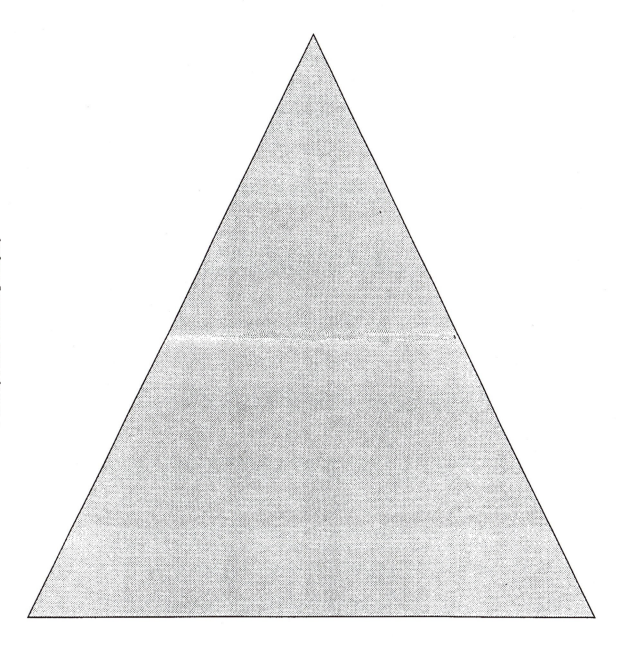

Form Shape Page

Form Shape Page

Form Shape Page

Music Forms Activity Page

Form	Graphic
Nocturne	
Theme and Variations	
Fugue	
Serenade	
Suite	
Rondo	

Meditation
(MASSENET)

Lesson Plan

Objective: Students will identify and perform the quarter note triplet (♩♩♩).

Materials: Piano
Copies of the Musical Excerpt from *Meditation*
Rhythm Cards
Copies of the Quarter-Note Triplet Activity Page
Rhythm Instruments

Procedure:
1. **Tell the story** of *Meditation* to the students.
2. **Teach the tune** to the students.
3. **Echo clap:**
   Do these numerous times until the students develop a feel for the rhythm.

   a)

   b)

4. **Focus the lesson** on the quarter note triplet ♩♩♩. Use the Rhythm Cards to assist in the defining of the rhythm. Have the class sing the tune and clap the three notes of the triplet rhythm on the words "opera by." Try stomping, snapping, or any other motion or movement to highlight and perform the rhythm.

5. **Activity:** This activity will help the students understand the value assigned to the quarter note triplet. Select a student to hold the Rhythm Card (♩♩♩). Have one or two students pick from a stack of rhythm cards to find a combination of rhythms that are equal in beat value to the ♩♩♩ rhythm. Continue this activity with the entire class.

Activity Page: Guide and lead the students through the exercises. Clapping, rhythm sticks, or drums can be rewarding while learning the rhythm.

Story of *Meditation* (Thais)

Jules Massenet was a French composer known for his great opera works. Among these were *Thais, Manon, Werther*, and *Our Lady's Juggler*.

The story has been told that Jules Massenet attended a performance of one of his operas, and he noticed that one of the singers sang flat throughout the entire work. After the performance was over, the singer confronted the composer for congratulations. He asked Massenet, "What did you think of my performance, Maestro?" Massenet replied, "You were wonderful, but the orchestra played sharp during the entire performance!"

Thais is a lyrical comedy which takes place in fourth century Egypt. The story centers around a woman, Thais, who is corrupted by the evils of the day. A man, Nathaniel, tries to convince her to go to the convent and turn her life around. Eventually, she heeds his advice, and by the end of the opera he shows his love for her.

Musical Excerpt from *Meditation*
(Thais)
JULES MASSENET (1842–1912)

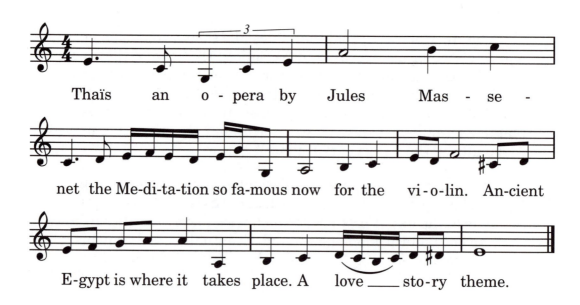

Thaïs an o-pera by Jules Mas-se-net the Me-di-ta-tion so fa-mous now for the vi-o-lin. An-cient E-gypt is where it takes place. A love ____ sto-ry theme.

Rhythm Card
Quarter Note Triplet

Quarter-Note Triplet Activity Page

* Try writing your own rhythm line. Remember: use at least one ♩♩♩ .

© 1997 by Parker Publishing Company

The Moldau
(SMETANA)

Lesson Plan

Objective: Students will identify and perform the meter of 6/8.

Materials: Piano
                    Copies of the Rhythm Cards
                    Copies of Rhythm Tab Cards Pages
                    Copies of 6/8 Meter Activity Page

Procedure: 1. ***Tell the story*** of *The Moldau* to the students.

                    2. ***Teach the tune*** to the students.

                    3. ***Echo clap and count*** the following rhythms with the students.

                    4. **Focus the lesson** on 6/8 meter. Use the Rhythm Cards to introduce and explain.

                    5. *Activity:* Use the rhythm tab pages. Each student needs a copy. Possibly have students cut the pieces out and put the the pieces in an envelope to store them for later use. Have each student use the tabs to compose his/her own 6/8 measure and lines.

Activity Page: Review the note values in 6/8 meter. Have the students clap or play and count the five exercises.

Follow-Up Activity: Sing a few familiar 6/8 tunes. Count and clap the rhythm of each tune. Also, play a few tunes with different meters (such as 4/4), including tunes in 6/8, so the students can guess which tunes are in 6/8.

Story of *The Moldau*

The Moldau was written by a Czechoslovakian composer named Smetana. He was considered a "nationalistic composer" because he wrote music expressing his nationalistic and political emotions for his country. Nationalistic music arrived during the uprisings and revolutions of the 1840s. One of Smetana's most famous works was the *The Moldau*. It is a tone poem (or program music—music meant to be heard after the audience reads about the story of it) about the famous Bohemian river in Smetana's fatherland called Czechoslovakia. The music begins slowly while picking up intensity as it flows into a strong and forceful river. The poem about the Moldau described how the river begins in the woods where sounds of the hunt and hunter's horns are heard and how it flows through the grassy pastures and fields and lowlands where a wedding feast is being celebrated by song and dance. The poem describes the night when the wood and the water fairies revel in the sparkling water. In the reflection of the water are castles of the historic knights who have vanished. The river then flows peacefully into the Czech capital of Prague. *The Moldau* was written in 1874 (by that time Smetana was deaf), one of six tone poems from a larger work called "My Fatherland." Each tone poem refers to a thing, a place, a historical fact, or a myth of the Czechoslovakian national heritage.

Musical Excerpt from *The Moldau* (My Fatherland)
BEDRICH SMETANA (1824–1884)

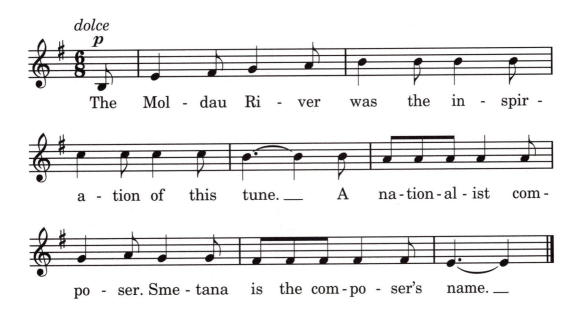

Rhythm Card: Eighth Note

Rhythm Card: Quarter Rest

Rhythm Card: Eighth-Note Triplet

Rhythm Tab Cards Page

$\frac{6}{8}$	$\frac{3}{8}$	$\frac{12}{8}$	$\frac{4}{4}$	$\frac{2}{4}$
$\frac{3}{4}$	C	¢	$\frac{6}{4}$	$\frac{2}{2}$
♪	♪	♪	♪	♪
♪	♪	♪	♩	♩
♩	♩	♩	♩	♩
♩.	♩.	♩.	♩.	♩.
𝅝.	𝅝.	𝅝.	♪♪♪	♪♪♪
♪♪♪	♪♪♪	♩·	♩·	♩·
♪	♪	♪	𝄽	𝄽

262

Rhythm Tab Cards Page

6/8 Meter Activity Page

6/8 Meter = six beats per measure
        an eighth note (♪) equals one beat.

Perform the 6/8 meter exercises below. Count and clap.

Tales from the Vienna Woods
(J. STRAUSS)

Lesson Plan

Objective: Students will identify and perform 3/8 meter.

Materials: Piano
Copies of the Meter Cards made from the Meter Cards Page
Copies of the Musical Excerpt from *Tales from the Vienna Woods*
Assorted music texts or books
Copies of the Waltz Activity Page

Procedure: 1. ***Tell the story*** of *Tales from the Vienna Woods* to the students.

2. ***Teach the tune*** to the students.

3. ***Echo clap*** the following:

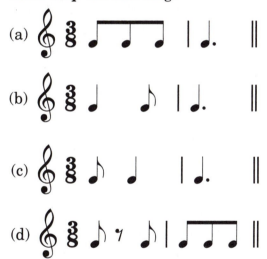

4. ***Focus the lesson*** on 3/8 meter. Use the Meter Cards to help you. Tell the students that the rhythms they clapped were in 3/8 meter. Then ask them, "What does that mean?"

5. ***Activity:*** Give each student a copy of the tune. Explain the grace note to the students. Have the students write out the rhythm counts below the notes of the tune.

Activity Page: Read and discuss the definition of a waltz. Have the students compose their own waltzes by using the note banks given for 3/8 meter. Be sure they begin and end on an "F." Play their compositions, so they get the satisfaction of hearing their own creations.

Story of *Tales from the Vienna Woods*

Johann Strauss, Jr. was the son of a popular musician of Vienna, Austria. Strauss's father allowed his son to study piano because it was the proper thing for well-educated and civilized people to do. However, Strauss, Jr. desired to do more than play just because it was the right thing to do. He wanted to play for his living.

The father's attempts to keep the son out of the music profession had a hidden motive. Strauss, Sr. didn't want competition from his son. As a result, a feud began between the father and the son.

Strauss, Sr. had his son "blackballed" or shut out of dance halls and concert halls in the city of Vienna, so Junior turned to the outskirts. One concert was arranged at a casino a few miles from Vienna. This event was advertised and promoted on the kiosks (round bulletin boards in the streets) of Vienna. The concert was sold out and so mobbed by people who wanted to attend and see the younger Strauss that the police were called in to keep order.

The concert was such a success that it raised Strauss, Jr. to stardom. As Junior's career took off, his father's career slowed down. Strauss, Jr. became known as the "Waltz King" because of his favoritism towards the waltz (perhaps due to his lifetime exposure to dancing and dance halls). Music brought him fame and adoration throughout the world for years.

Johann Strauss, Jr. composed 479 orchestral works and more than nine dozen operas during his career. His love for his home of Vienna and Austria inspired many of his works, including *Tales from the Vienna Woods*. In 1899, on his way home from a concert, Strauss, Jr. caught a chill and developed pneumonia. Soon afterwards, he died. His grave in Vienna lies near the graves of Beethoven, Schubert, and Brahms, in good company with the great composers.

© 1997 by Parker Publishing Company

Musical Excerpt
from *Tales from the Vienna Woods*
JOHANN STRAUSS, JR. (1825–1899)

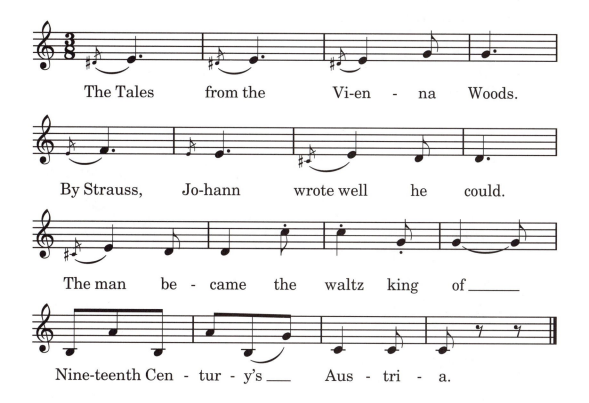

The Tales   from the   Vi-en - na   Woods.

By Strauss,   Jo-hann   wrote well   he   could.

The man   be - came   the   waltz   king   of ____

Nine-teenth Cen - tur - y's ___   Aus - tri - a.

Meter Cards Page

Name _____

Waltz Activity Page

The Waltz

Johann Strauss, Jr. was considered the "Waltz King." What is the waltz? The waltz is a dance intended for two people, or a couple dance. It is in triple time (i.e. 3/8, 3/4, 3/2). The waltz has been a popular dance since the 1700s, and remains popular with ballroom dancers today.

Using the tonal and rhythm banks below, write your own waltz. Begin and end on the note "**F**".

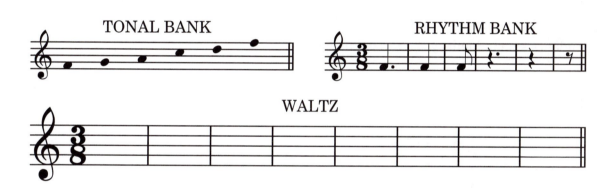

Classic Tunes Level V Quiz
Teacher's Edition

Directions: Play the following tunes in the order given. Students are to identify the tunes and their composers

TUNE	COMPOSER
1. *Liebestraum*	*Liszt*
2. *Unfinished Symphony*	*Schubert*
3. *La Gioconda*	*Ponchielli*
4. *Tales from the Vienna Woods*	*Strauss*
5. *Meditation*	*Massenet*
6. *The Moldau*	*Smetana*

Students should identify the meters as follows:

1. 6/8	*Compound*	5.	12/8	*Compound*
2. 2/4	*Duple*	6.	4/4	*Compound*
3. 3/4	*Triple*	7.	C	*Compound*
4. 5/4	*Compound*	8.	2/2	*Duple*

© 1997 by Parker Publishing Company

Name _____

Classic Tunes Level V Quiz

Listening: Identify the following tunes and composers.

TUNE	*COMPOSER*
1. _____	_____
2. _____	_____
3. _____	_____
4. _____	_____
5. _____	_____

Identify the following meters as duple, triple, or compound.

1. 6/8	_____	5.	12/8	_____
2. 2/4	_____	6.	4/4	_____
3. 3/4	_____	7.	C	_____
4. 5/4	_____	8.	2/2	_____

Unfinished Symphony
(SCHUBERT)

Lesson Plan

Objective: Students will identify and perform duple, triple, and compound meters.

Materials: Piano
Meter Cards made from Meter Term Cards Page
Copies of the Meter Activity Page
Rhythm Tab Cards (from *The Moldau* lesson)

Procedure:

1. ***Tell the story*** of the *Unfinished Symphony* to the students.

2. ***Teach the tune*** to the students.

3. ***Focus the lesson*** on meter, using the Meter Cards. Define the following terms to the students. Also, explain that there are essentially two kinds of meter: duple and triple. **Duple meter**: meter based on two beats. **Triple meter**: meter based on three beats. **Compound meter**: a combination of duple or triple meter. **Quadruple meter**: 4/4 meter can be considered quadruple; however, it is a compound duple meter.

4. ***Explain*** how 6/8 or 4/4, etc. works as a compound meter—a group of triple or duple meters.

5. ***Activity:*** Display a variety of meters: 2/4, 4/4, 5/4, 3/4, 6/4, 3/8, 6/8, 9/8, 12/8, C, ¢, 2/2, and 3/2 (use Meter Cards). Arrange students in pairs. Have one student identify the meter as duple or triple or compound. The partner will decide if the other is correct. Finally, the class will let the partner know which it is by signaling two fingers for duple, three fingers for triple, or form a "C" with one hand for compound.

6. ***Activity:*** Using the Rhythm Tab Card from *The Moldau* lesson plan, have the students construct a measure containing a variety of meters. You may want to tell them which meter (duple, triple, or compound).

Activity Page: On the first section, have the students identify the meters as duple, triple, or compound. The second section example should have the meter filled in by the students.

Answer Key: Meter Activity Page
Triple, Quadruple, Compound, Duple; $\frac{3}{4} \bullet \frac{5}{4} \bullet \frac{9}{8}$

Story of the *Unfinished Symphony*

When Franz Schubert was about 25 years old, he began to compose his 8th Symphony in B minor; however, only two movements, or parts, were completed. It is believed that he did plan on composing an entire symphony because sketches of a third movement were found. After Schubert's death, a composer finished the symphony in the style and true voice of the lyrical writing of the original composer.

Schubert found the inspiration for his compositions from many sources. One day, a friend came to visit him when the composer was not in the mood for work. They decided to have some coffee, so Schubert proceeded to prepare it. He measured the beans and placed them in the grinder. He soon exclaimed, "I've got it! I've got it! You old coffee grinder, you." He shoved the grinder back in the corner. His friend asked, "Franz, what have you got?" Schubert replied "This coffee grinder is a wonderful thing. Melodies and themes come spouting out, that's what. It is the noise and sounds of the machine that give a composer who has not been able to come up with an idea for days some inspiration." He began humming and singing tunes that soon became one of his string quartets.

Musical Excerpt
from the *Unfinished Symphony* No. 8
FRANZ SCHUBERT (1797–1828)

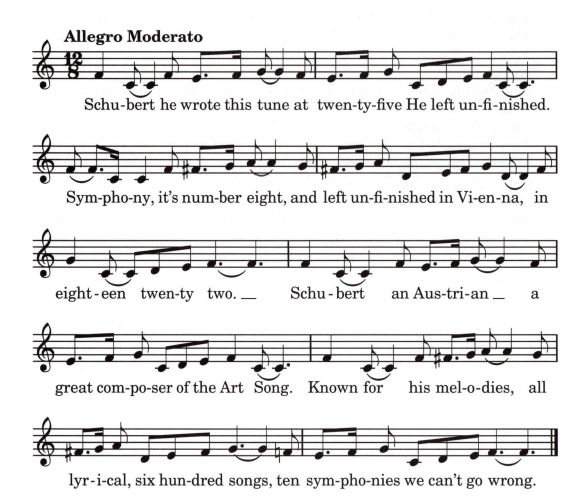

Allegro Moderato

Schu-bert he wrote this tune at twen-ty-five He left un-fi-nished.

Sym-pho-ny, it's num-ber eight, and left un-fi-nished in Vi-en-na, in

eight-een twen-ty two. __ Schu-bert an Aus-tri-an __ a

great com-po-ser of the Art Song. Known for his mel-o-dies, all

lyr-i-cal, six hun-dred songs, ten sym-pho-nies we can't go wrong.

DUPLE

TRIPLE

COMPOUND

METER

Meter Activity Page

Meters: duple, triple, and compound

Identify the following as duple, triple, quadruple, or compound meter.

Meters: Missing meters

Fill in the correct meter of the following exercises.

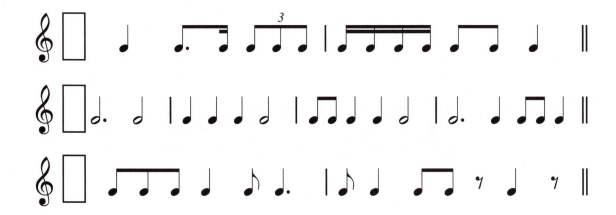

Water Music Suite
(HANDEL)

Lesson Plan

Objective: Students will identify characteristics, events, and people from the Baroque and Renaissance periods of music.

Materials: Piano
Musical Excerpts of Renaissance and Baroque music
Copies of the Style Period Cards
Copies of the Music Periods Activity Page

Procedure:
1. ***Tell the story*** of *Water Music* to the students.
2. ***Teach the tune*** to the students.
3. ***Focus the lesson*** on the Baroque and Renaissance styles of music.
4. ***Activity:*** Read and discuss the Renaissance/Baroque Periods Pages. Ask and discuss the following questions, "When was this period?" "What historical events occurred during this time?" "Who were some of the notable people, musical or nonmusical?" "What were some of the characteristics of the style?"

Activity Page: Students should classify the Music Era Bank terms, tunes, composers, events, notables, etc., into the correct era category.

Follow-Up Activity: Group students into teams of two or three. Play a variety of music excerpts from the Baroque and Renaissance periods (recordings or tunes). Ask the students to decide why these pieces are considered Baroque or Renaissance. Possibly, play a few Romantic and Modern pieces for the students to explain why they aren't representative of the focus periods. Later, play a few more examples of Baroque and Renaissance music, and have the students decide which period the examples best represent. Put the class together and have a worthwhile discussion of the styles.

Answer Key: Music Periods Activity Page

Renaissance: individual, 1400–1600, fewer rules, more dissonance, Dante, Henry VIII, Monteverdi, Modern Age, printing press, Dufay, Columbus

Baroque: polyphonic, Age of Reason, oratorio, ornamental, individual, Handel, fugue, 1600–1750, Vivaldi, Bach, Michelangelo, more rules, suite, opera.

Story of the *Water Music Suite*

London is where George Handel composed the *Water Music Suite* in 1717, when the royal family and members of the nobility took part in a royal party on barges floating on the River Thames. For this event, Handel created music for a large orchestra of over fifty musicians.

Handel was born in Halle, Germany, the son of a barber-surgeon who did not regard music as a suitable profession for a middle-class person. Nonetheless, Handel entered the world of music forever. He spent time working in Germany and Italy until 1710 when he took a trip to London, a city which would become his home for fifty years. While in London, Handel worked for King George I, feuded with fellow composers, lost money while trying to produce unsuccessful operas, and composed some of his greatest music including the *Messiah*, the *Royal Fireworks Suite*, and the *Water Music*. After becoming blind from cataracts and suffering from numerous debilitating strokes, Handel died at the age of 64.

Musical Excerpt
from the *Water Music Suite* (Hornpipe)
G. F. HANDEL (1685–1759)

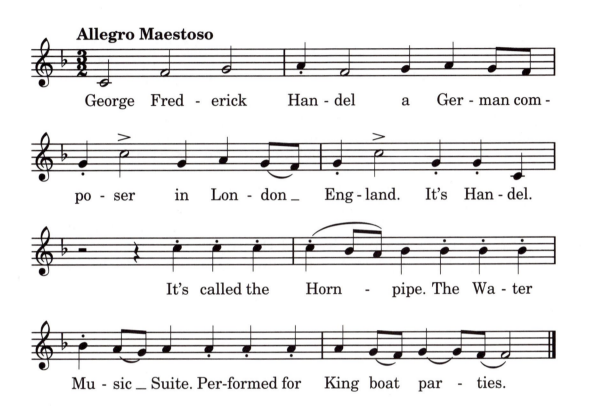

Renaissance Period

The Renaissance Period occurred from 1400 to 1600, between the Middle Ages and the Baroque Period. The word Renaissance means "rebirth." It was meant to represent the rebirth of the individual and was characterized by new emphasis on individual thought and belief and discovery, dawn of the age of science, and the beginning of the modern age. The roots of the Renaissance lie in the Italian 14th century when society revived ancient classical learning.

Musically, the Renaissance provided fewer rules and inhibitions—more dissonance (clashing sounds), more chromaticism, imitation, homophonic and monophonics, music printing, and music written exclusively for instruments. Key musical figures of the period included Dufay, Desprey, Monteverdi, and Frescobaldi.

Major historical events and figures of the Renaissance period were Columbus's discovery of America (1492), end of the Hundred Years' War (1453), War of the Roses (1455), Spanish Inquisition (1478), Donatello (artist), Richard III, Henry VIII, Shakespeare, Gutenberg (printing press), Dante (writer), and Leonardo da Vinci.

Baroque Period

The Baroque Period appeared soon after the Renaissance and covers the years from 1600 to 1750. The term Baroque comes from a Portuguese word meaning "a pearl of irregular shape." Baroque Period culture reflected a novel approach to turning human emotions into art.

Baroque music is basically homophonic. However, polyphonic music began to sprout and flourish during the Baroque era. The music is expressive and ornamental, and the dissonance is more controlled. The individualism and emotionalism of this period was accompanied by more rules (The Age of Reason).

Composers of the Baroque era included Handel, Bach, Vivaldi, Scarlatti, Purcell, and Telemann. Musical forms involved during this period included opera, the oratorio, the suite, the fugue, the sonata, and the concerto.

Some major historical figures and events of the Baroque Period are Isaac Newton (inventor) Galileo (scientist), Rembrandt (artist), Raphael (artist), Michelangelo (artist), the settlement of Plymouth Colony by the Pilgrims (1620), the first Thanksgiving (1621), and the first publication of *Poor Richard's Almanac* by Benjamin Franklin (1732).

Style Period Cards

RENAISSANCE

BAROQUE

CLASSICAL

ROMANTIC

MODERN

CONTEMPORARY

IMPRESSIONIST

Name _____

Music Periods Activity Page

Using the Musical Era Bank, identify the terms, events, names, etc., as related to the Renaissance or Baroque Periods and place the corresponding characteristics or people in the spaces below.

RENAISSANCE	**BAROQUE**
_____	_____
_____	_____
_____	_____
_____	_____
_____	_____
_____	_____
_____	_____
_____	_____
_____	_____
_____	_____

MUSICAL ERA BANK

Individual	fewer rules and inhibitions	more rules
more dissonance	polyphony flourished	Columbus
Age of Reason	Modern Age began	opera
oratorio	Henry VIII	Michelangelo
ornamental	Monteverdi	Bach
Handel	Printing press	fugue
suite	Vivaldi	Dufay
Dante	1400–1600	1600–1750

283

La Traviata
(Verdi)

Lesson Plan

Objective: Students will identify characteristics, major events, and people of the Classical and Romantic Periods.

Materials: Piano
Copies of Classical and Romantic Period Pages
Listening examples of Verdi and Mozart
Copies of the Music Styles Comparison page

Procedure:

1. ***Tell the story*** of *La Traviata* to the students.

2. ***Teach the tune*** to the students.

3. ***Focus the lesson*** on the Romantic and Classical Periods. Explain that Verdi was a Romantic composer of opera and Mozart was a Classical opera composer. The intent of the lesson, partially, is to compare the two periods of culture. A good comparison activity is to play a variety of Classical and Romantic music excerpts and discuss the differences between the two styles. Another way to compare is to play excerpts from a Mozart opera and a Verdi opera (possibly, use the overtures) and make observations about the text, instrumentation, etc.

4. ***Activity:*** Divide the class into eight teams. Assign two teams either musical characteristics, philosophical characteristics, composers and their music, and famous figures and historical events. Give each team copies of the Romantic and Classical Periods pages. Have the students read and synthesize the information and facts on the Period page, and make a comparison of the two styles in regards to their assigned topic and record the findings on the Comparison Team Page. After the teams have finished, have the teams present their findings to the class.

Activity Page: Have the students use the Classical and Romantic Periods pages to assist them in a comparison writing. They need to address the characteristics of the philosophy of the periods, the musical characteristics, the historical facts and figures, and the composers and their music.

Story of *La Traviata* (The Wayward Woman)

La Traviata is set in Paris during the 1800s. It begins at the home of Violetta, a beautiful and celebrated courtesan, where a party is taking place. Alfred, a party guest, is a man who had come to visit Violetta every day during her recent illness to find out how she was doing. Alfred sings a toast of love to Violetta.

After the guests go off to dance, Violetta collapses in a coughing fit. She insists it is nothing. Nevertheless, Alfred declares his love for Violetta. She laughs, saying that she has only a few months to live. However, she is touched by his love. She makes a proposal to him that when the camelia she has given him has faded, he may return to her.

The guests leave, and Violetta considers Alfred's offer of love. But she decides to continue her lavish life of parties. Later, she changes her mind and decides to pursue Alfred, and the couple become blissfully happy. Then, one day Alfred's father comes to see Violetta to tell her that she must break up with his son in order to avoid a scandal. Violetta's lifestyle is quite well-known, but not well-regarded.

Violetta does as Alfred's father asks, but Alfred becomes enraged and storms away from Violetta, leaving her sobbing. However, Alfred soon finds out what his father did and decides to return to Violetta. But before returning, he notices that the camelia that Violetta had given him has faded. He immediately returns to Violetta and declares his love again. But when he arrives, he finds her dying. Alfred's father realizes the mistake he has made by breaking up the couple, but it is too late. Violetta dies.

Musical Excerpt from *La Traviata*
(Brandisi)
G. VERDI (1813–1901)

Classical Period

The Classical Period spanned the years of 1700 to 1800. It overlaps the end of the Baroque (Rococo) and the beginning of the Romantic Periods. The term classical stems from Greek-Roman tradition with characteristics like balance, even proportion, simplicity, poise, disciplined craftsmanship, and objective expression. When we think of a classic, we refer to excellence and quality. The musical innovations include simple homophonic texture, crescendo and decrescendo dynamics, the overture, a more advanced solo concerto, and the symphony. Hadyn, Mozart, and early Beethoven were the eminent composers of the period. George Washington, Ben Franklin, Thomas Jefferson, Napoleon, King George III, Goethe, Declaration of Independence, French Revolution, and the Boston Tea Party are some of the major figures and events of the Classical Period.

Romantic Period

The Romantic Period extended from 1800 to about 1900. The word romantic is derived from romance. The Romantic movement broke away from the rules and discipline of the Classical period. It is based in the mystical and characterized by strong emotion, vivid imagery, and uncontrolled creative imagination of the individual.

Musically, some works became lengthy and experimented with tonality and texture. Music was created to symbolize and signify emotion, greatness, and literature (the symphonic poem), putting the nonmusical into music. Robert Schumann, Brahms, Beethoven, Liszt, Wagner, Chopin, Schubert, Berlioz, Mendelssohn, and Strauss were some of the great Romantic composers.

Some major figures and events of the Romantic Period were Abraham Lincoln, Thomas Edison, Karl Marx, George Eliot, Sigmund Freud, *Moby Dick*, the Civil War, the Gold Rush, and the construction of railroads and development of the oil industry.

Classical and Romantic Periods Comparison

Team Members

_____

_____

_____

_____

Topic

_____

Comparison of Styles

Classical

Romantic

Music Styles Comparison

Using the Classical and Romantic Periods pages, write a comparison between the two styles. Be sure to discuss philosophy, musical characteristics, historical events and figures, and composers and their music.

Bolero
(RAVEL)

Lesson Plan

Objective: Students will identify characteristics, major events, and people of the Impressionist and Modern/Contemporary Periods.

Materials: Piano
Copies of the Impressionist and Modern Facts Page
Copies of the Music Period Descriptions page

Procedure: 1. ***Tell the story*** of *Bolero* to the students.

2. ***Teach the tune*** to the students.

3. ***Focus the lesson*** on the Impressionist, Modern, and Contemporary Periods.

4. ***Activity:*** Use the Impressionist and Modern Facts Page to assist students in discussing the essential elements of the periods as a whole class or in groups.

Activity Page: Have the students use the Facts Page to assist them in writing a description of both the Impressionist and Modern/Contemporary Periods.

Follow-Up Activity: Find examples of artwork from the different periods and styles and discuss the similarities to its music counterparts.

Composition Activity: Allow the students to use a variety of rhythm and tonal instruments to compose a piece of contemporary music. Have the students write it down in their own notation so they can perform it for the class. Perhaps, allow others to try reading others' notation.

Story of *Bolero*

Ravel's success as a composer began in the early 1900s. His career was interrupted by the First World War. Being an extremely small man, he was not able to serve in the army. But, he finally succeeded in joining the war effort by becoming an ambulance driver. After the war, he became internationally successful, and he toured as often as his frail health would allow.

After much persuasion, Ravel visited America in 1928. He was an instant success. His music, which he conducted and performed on the piano, overwhelmed the public.

However, an illness became more burdensome, and, eventually, fatal. In the summer of 1937, he suffered an attack while returning home from a gala performance of his ballet *Daphne and Chloe*. He never recovered, dying in December of the same year.

Bolero is a repetitive piece that brought great fame to Ravel. During the premiere of the piece, a woman yelled out "He's mad!" Ravel was later heard to say, "Ah, she understands the piece."

Musical Excerpt from *Bolero*
MAURICE RAVEL (1875–1937)

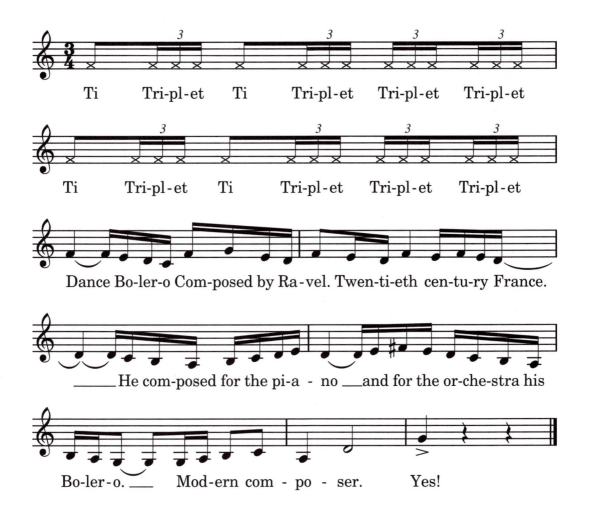

Ti Tri-pl-et Ti Tri-pl-et Tri-pl-et Tri-pl-et

Ti Tri-pl-et Ti Tri-pl-et Tri-pl-et Tri-pl-et

Dance Bo-ler-o Com-posed by Ra-vel. Twen-ti-eth cen-tu-ry France.

_____ He com-posed for the pi-a - no _____and for the or-che-stra his

Bo-ler-o. ___ Mod-ern com - po - ser. Yes!

Impressionist/Modern Facts Page

IMPRESSIONISTIC

— 1875 to 1925

— Impressionism was introduced in the visual arts referring to blurred images.

— Suffused effects of light, color, and atmospheric conditions.

— Claude Debussy was the critical composer.

— Painters: Monet and Manet.

— Musically: complex textures, non-climatic melodies, color-oriented (usage of particular instrumental colors).

— Events: World War I, Mexican-American War, and Panama Canal.

— People: Theodore Roosevelt and Woodrow Wilson.

MODERN/CONTEMPORARY

— 1900 to Today

— Collapse of the Tonal System of the 18th and 19th centuries.

— New compositional possibilities due to the end of compositional limitations.

— Twelve-tone system, Serial Music, electronic music, Jazz, Rock, Minimalism (Glass), Microtonal music (John Eaton), and Expressionism.

— Composers: Penderecki, Stockhausen, Boulez, Ravel, Berg, Schoeberg, Webern, Cowell, Partch, Varese, Cage, and Babbit.

— Neo-Classical composers: Stravinsky, Bartok, Prokofiev, Copland, and Hindemith.

— Distortion

— Events: World War II, Korean War, computers, and Vietnam War.

— People: Eisenhower, Churchill, Hitler, and Patton.

Music Period Descriptions

Using the Facts Pages, write a paragraph or two describing the Impressionist and Modern/Contemporary Periods.

Impressionist Period

Modern/Contemporary Periods

Grand Canyon Suite
(GROFÉ)

Lesson Plan

Objective: Students will recognize and identify key signatures.

Materials: Piano
Copies of the Key Signature Cards
Copies of *Grand Canyon Suite* Excerpts
Copies of Sharp Keys Activity Page
Copies of Key Signatures Song Search Page

Procedure:
1. **Tell the story** of *Grand Canyon Suite* to the students.
2. **Teach the tune** to the students.
3. **Focus the lesson** on key signatures. Use the Key Signature Cards to help you explain to the students how to recognize sharp keys. They need to realize that key signatures are important to musicians, because the key notifies the player what needs to be done in order to play the music. Demonstrate how you take the last sharp written and go to the letter that follows it to find the name of the major key. Run a few examples using the key signature cards. Also, students need to realize when you have the key of "C" (think "C" Level)—sharps go above the surface of the sea and flats go below. You can explain at a later time that there are minor keys.
4. **Activity:** Using the excerpts from the *Grand Canyon Suite*, have the students figure out the keys to each movement.

Activity Page: Students are to write in the name of the key for part I. In part II, students will write out the sharps for each key name given.

Follow-Up Lesson/Activity: To teach the flat keys, use the Key Signature Cards to help explain that one takes the next to last flat written to find the key.

Next to last flat. Key of B flat.

One More Activity: Have the students search in various music books to find songs in flat keys or both flat and sharp keys. The titles of the songs could be recorded on the Key Signatures Song Search Page. This can be done individually or in groups. You might group the students into teams. Assign each team a key signature. Allow them to search for as many songs as possible in their particular key.

Answer Key: Sharp Keys Activity Page
Keys of: D, E, C, B; *C* = No Sharps. *E* = F#, C#, G#, D#. *B* = F#, C#, G#, D#, A#. *D* = F#, C#.

Story of *Grand Canyon Suite*

The *Grand Canyon Suite* was first conceived by Grofé during a vacation in Arizona in the 1920s. The suite is made up of five descriptive movements: Sunrise, Painted Desert, On the Trail, Sunset, and Cloudburst.

The Sunrise describes a quiet, peaceful rising sun on a beautiful day in the vast, spacious canyon. The Painted Desert movement depicts the lonely grandeur of the spacious arid land. On the Trail was inspired by the noise of a pile driver outside a hotel room in Chicago with the rocking of his son's baby carriage creating the clippity-clop sounds of the mules on the trail. The fourth movement, Sunset, came to the composer while he was playing a round of golf. Finally, the suite ends with the music Grofé experienced during a thunderstorm while staying in Germany. Cloudburst demonstrates the violence and power of a Grand Canyon storm.

Ferdé Grofé, an American composer, was known predominantly for his pieces *The Grand Canyon Suite* and *El Salon de Mexico*.

Musical Excerpt
from *Grand Canyon Suite*
FERDÉ GROFÉ (1892–1972)

Clip - di-clop clip - di-clop   clip - di-clop On the Trail

Clip - di-clop clip - di-clop   clip - di-clop On the Trail _

Fer - de _____   Gro - fé _____   com -

posed this piece ___ called Grand Can-yon   Suite. _____

298

Other Excerpts: *Grand Canyon Suite*
FERDÉ GROFÉ (1892–1972)

Sunrise

Painted Desert

On the Trail

Sunset

Key Signature Card: C

Key of C

Key Signature Cards: D & G

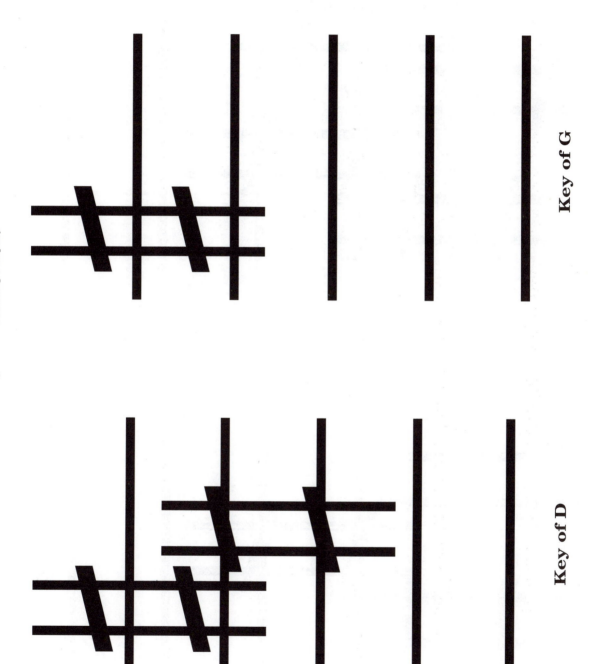

Key of G

Key of D

301

Key Signature Cards: A & E

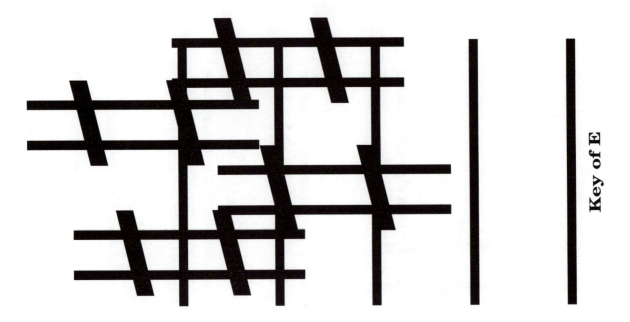

Key of E

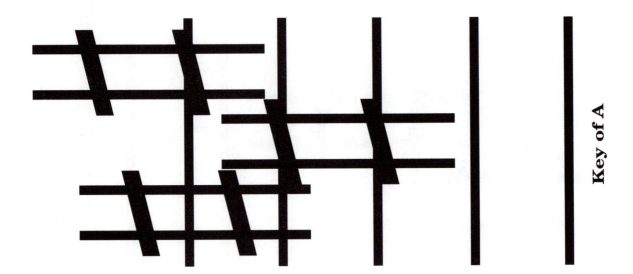

Key of A

Key Signature Card: B

Key of B

303

Key Signature Card: F#

Key of F#

Key Signature Cards: F & B♭

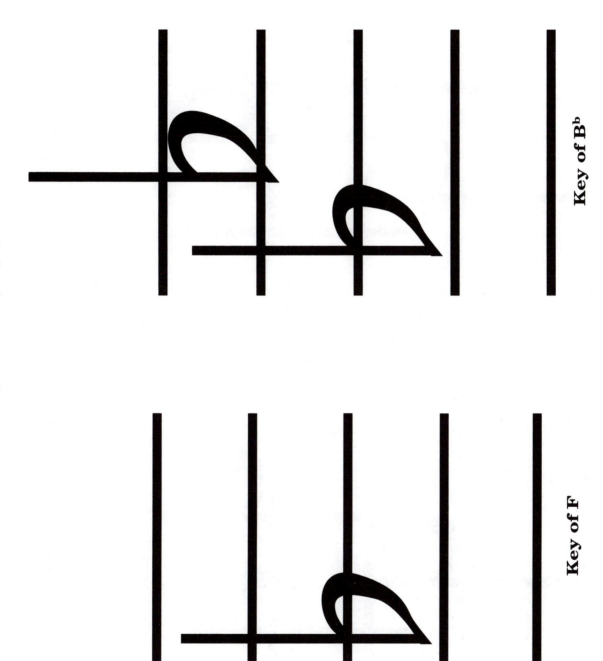

Key of B♭

Key of F

Key Signature Cards: E♭ & A♭

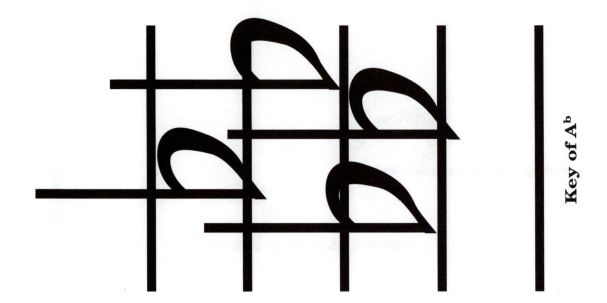

Key of A♭

Key of E♭

Key Signature Card: D♭

Key of D♭

Key Signature Card: G♭

Key of G♭

© 1997 by Parker Publishing Company

Name _____

Sharp Keys Activity Page

Identify the following keys. *Remember:* Find the last sharp written in the key signature. Then take that letter and go to the following letter in the alphabet.

Example: F#

Next letter in the alphabet is "G." They key is "G."

Key of: _____   _____   _____   _____

Label the sharps of the following keys. The order of the sharps will follow the sentence: Fat Cats Go Down Alleys Everywhere, Buster.

Key of: C   E   B   D

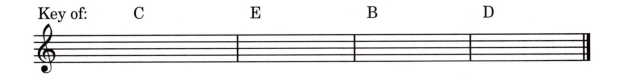

Key Signatures Song Search Page

Directions: Write the titles of the songs you find that match the particular keys below.

Key of F
_____
_____
_____

Key of B Flat
_____
_____

Key of E Flat
_____
_____

Key of A Flat
_____
_____

Key of C
_____
_____

Key of G
_____
_____

Key of D
_____
_____

Key of A
_____
_____

Key of E
_____
_____

Classic Tunes Level V Test
(Teacher's Edition)

Directions: Give students copies of the following student test page for Level V. For Part 1, Listening, play musical excerpts from the ten compositions in Level V in any order you wish and have students write each title and the composer's name in the order they are played. For Part II, Key Signatures, students are to identify each of the five keys.

I. *Listening*

Write the title and the composer's name to the tunes you hear in the spaces given below.

Title   Composer

1. _____   _____

2. _____   _____

3. _____   _____

4. _____   _____

5. _____   _____

6. _____   _____

7. _____   _____

8. _____   _____

9. _____   _____

10. _____   _____

II. *Key Signatures*

Identify the following keys.

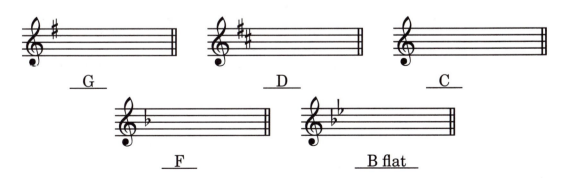

G   D   C

F   B flat

Name _____

Classic Tunes Level V Test

I. *Listening*
   Write the title and the composer's name to the tunes you hear in the spaces given below.

   Title   Composer

   1. _____   _____

   2. _____   _____

   3. _____   _____

   4. _____   _____

   5. _____   _____

   6. _____   _____

   7. _____   _____

   8. _____   _____

   9. _____   _____

   10. _____   _____

II. *Key Signatures*
    Identify the following keys.

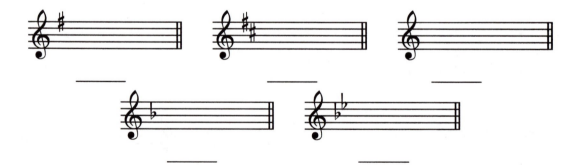

SUPPLEMENTARY MATERIALS

Classic Tunes for the Recorder

"Surprise" Symphony

Ode to Joy

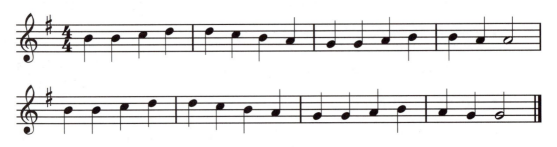

Fire Bird

Trumpet Voluntary

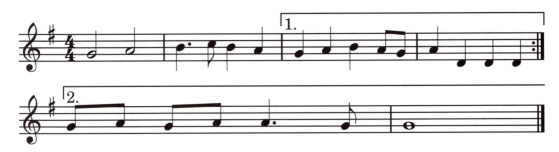

314

The Trout

Canon

Fantasie-Impromptu

Largo

Classic Tunes & Tales Games

CTBS Interview

Objective: Students will review composer facts.

Materials: Paper and pencil for each interviewer

Procedure: Select one student to be the Classic Tune Broadcast System interviewer and one student as any composer. The interviewer asks questions of the composer, and both the composer and interviewer write an article about the composer. The students need to remember tunes, tales, and any other information available to complete the project.

Who Am I?

Objective: Students will review facts about composers.

Materials: Composer cards

Procedure: Have one student select a composer card and pretend to be that composer. Another student (or whole class) asks the composer questions. They can only ask "yes" or "no" answer questions. After a number of questions, the class may guess the identity of the composer.

Question Examples:
        Are you a ballet composer?
        Are you from Germany?
        Did you compose *Rigoletto*?

Classic Tune Detective Agency

Objective: Students will learn and review the lives of composers through discovery and deduction.

Materials: Envelope; a letter to or from the chosen composer; wallet; and various art supplies

Procedure: You will need to create five stations.

Station 1:   Prepare an envelope with a letter to or from the composer you are focusing on. You need to compose a letter that will contain information that will help students figure out their assigned composer.

Station 2:   You will need to prepare a concert program. Do not include the composer's name—only the music pieces, concert hall, date, city, etc.

Station 3:   Prepare a wallet with valuable information (e.g. wife's first name, money or no money, pictures, and other vital personal information).

Station 4:   Draw a map of the composer's home city.

Station 5:   Create a Hall of Records. In that hall students will find a folder with the composer's address, birth certificate, death certificate, etc.

Game Procedure: Pick teams with five students each. Each student will be assigned a station to go to and decipher information. Each student returns to his/her team and reports the discovered facts. The team must use all the facts discovered to determine the mystery composer. Allow 5–10 minutes for students to attend the station and return to their team. Keep a record of what teams discovered their composer. Continue the game throughout the school year using other composers. You can make it competitive by making a win list. The team with the most discoveries wins.

Select-a-Tune

Objective: Students will review tune titles and composers.

Materials: Title and composer cards (make a variety of composer and title cards.) *Examples:*

Mozart   *Swan Lake*

Procedure: Put the students in pairs. Give each pair a set of composer and title cards. Each student pulls a random card. Whether title or composer, one student tells the other what it is, and the other student guesses the name of the composer of the title or names the title of the composer. If the player is correct he keeps the card. If the player is incorrect, the card goes on the discard pile. The player with the most cards wins.

Classic Tunes & Tales Game Show

Objective: Students will review composers, terms, and other music elements.

Materials: Various questions (see Sample Questions)
Category Cards
Chalkboard
Piano

Procedure: *Preparation:*

You can leave the squares of each category blank and read the question, or you can use sheets of paper with the point amount each question is worth on the front and the question on the back (hidden). Tape each question to the appropriate square on the grid.

Game Play:

The game is more effective when played with teams. Select a student to choose a category and point level. Remember, the higher the point, the more difficult the question. If the student misses the question, it will be the student on the other team's turn to play. If one student correctly answers the question, add the points to their team's total. If neither student answers it correctly, no one receives a point—Then, rotate to the next player. Continue the game until all the questions have been selected. The team with the most points wins.

Alternate: You may choose to use this game at different levels. If so, you will need to write the appropriate level questions.

Sample Game Show Questions

	Notation	Composers	Listening	Instruments	Terms	Symbols
1	Name this note. (C)	Who wrote *Eine Kleine Nachtmusik?* (Mozart)	Name this tune. *Play: (William Tell Overture)*	Name an instrument family. (Brass, Woodwinds, Strings, Percussion)	What does "tempo" mean? (speed of the music)	What does this symbol mean? (repeat)
2	How many beats does this note receive? (3)	Which composer went deaf? (Beethoven)	Who wrote this tune? *Play: (Ode to Joy)*	What are the four families of instruments of the orchestra? (Brass, Woodwinds, Strings, Percussion)	Define the term "allegro." (fast, lively)	Name this symbol. > (accent)
3	What kind of note is this? (Eighth)	Name a Russian ballet composer. (Tchaikovsky, Stravinsky)	This tune is from what ballet? *Play: (Swan Lake)*	Name a double-reed instrument. (oboe, bassoon, English horn)	Name four dynamics terms in Italian. (Piano, Forte, Mezzo-piano, Mezzo-forte, pianissimo, fortissimo)	What does this symbol tell the performer? (staccato/short sound)
4	Which of these two notes is shorter?	Which Viennese composer was competitive with his father? (Johann Strauss, Jr.)	Who composed this tune? *Play: (Symphonie Fantastique)*	What is a "Sousaphone"? (Marching tuba, requested by Sousa)	Define "ritardando." (gradually slow down)	Name this symbol: (crescendo)
5	Write or draw a set of triplets.	Name 3 works by Mozart. *(Don Giovanni, Symphony No. 40, Eine Kleine Nachtmusik)*	Name this tune. *Play: (Symphony No. 2, Rachmaninoff)*	What is the lowest-sounding instrument in the orchestra? (contrabassoon)	What is a canon? (a kind of round)	What is this symbol? (a grace note)

Other possible categories: Form, Rhythm, Dynamics

319

Game Show Category Grid

Symbols	Terms	Instruments	Listening	Composers	Notation
1	1	1	1	1	1
2	2	2	2	2	2
3	3	3	3	3	3
4	4	4	4	4	4
5	5	5	5	5	5

Points

Classic Tune Game Show

Blank Question Grid

Category Points				
1				
2				
3				
4				
5				

321

Classic Tunes Ballet Wordsearch

B	T	U	O	D	B	B	F	S	D	S	Y	G	L	B	M	E	D	E	A
A	V	D	B	N	H	A	P	S	X	Y	K	U	E	F	A	V	J	Q	E
K	M	R	V	T	F	R	V	U	M	V	S	E	S	R	E	R	T	D	F
C	O	K	U	J	D	Y	F	E	A	I	V	C	S	Q	N	X	B	H	E
R	S	K	O	T	I	S	N	P	R	A	O	Y	Y	C	M	Z	D	E	P
S	A	Q	O	N	J	H	O	X	Q	Q	K	V	L	V	U	V	H	D	R
L	T	V	H	Q	Y	N	Y	K	W	C	I	H	P	X	R	I	E	E	T
S	M	R	E	Q	B	I	C	U	H	G	A	G	H	X	T	Y	W	X	P
N	W	X	A	L	N	K	N	O	H	W	H	L	I	Y	X	K	O	X	V
F	U	A	G	V	F	O	V	U	P	Q	C	R	D	C	A	N	C	A	N
C	D	Z	N	I	I	V	Z	W	R	L	T	E	E	V	G	N	X	C	H
R	N	M	C	L	G	N	G	H	X	E	A	C	O	P	P	E	L	I	A
T	O	M	G	B	A	X	S	N	X	Z	Y	N	D	J	F	K	R	R	H
R	L	B	Z	V	N	K	I	K	B	I	C	E	D	E	F	H	P	J	L
T	I	O	L	A	Y	A	E	W	Y	Q	P	L	V	R	M	P	T	Z	Q
G	U	D	C	O	U	R	D	E	B	A	L	L	E	T	O	I	V	D	M
A	C	R	L	N	U	T	C	R	A	C	K	E	R	S	M	D	L	Y	O
R	O	M	E	O	A	N	D	J	U	L	I	E	T	Z	D	N	E	L	H
E	Y	Q	K	B	I	L	L	Y	T	H	E	K	I	D	I	L	Z	O	E
A	P	P	A	L	A	C	H	I	A	N	S	P	R	I	N	G	T	C	Q

1. BARYSHNIKOV	2. NUREYEV
3. COURDEBALLET	4. SWANLAKE
5. NUTCRACKER	6. LESSYLPHIDE
7. ROMEOANDJULIET	8. RODEO
9. BILLYTHEKID	10. APPALACHIANSPRING
11. BARBER	12. RAVEL
13. COPLAND	14. COPPELIA
15. MEDEA	16. DEMILLE
17. SYVIA	18. CANCAN
19. TCHAIKOVSKY	20. STRAVINSKY

Classic Tunes Ballet Wordsearch
Answer Key

1. BARYSHNIKOV
2. NUREYEV
3. COURDEBALLET
4. SWANLAKE
5. NUTCRACKER
6. LESSYLPHIDE
7. ROMEOANDJULIET
8. RODEO
9. BILLYTHEKID
10. APPALACHIANSPRING
11. BARBER
12. RAVEL
13. COPLAND
14. COPPELIA
15. MEDEA
16. DEMILLE
17. SYVIA
18. CANCAN
19. TCHAIKOVSKY
20. STRAVINSKY

Classic Tunes & Tales
Composers Wordsearch No. 2

B	J	K	A	P	M	D	S	V	R	N	P	X	L	S	G	E	L	E	N
V	E	Q	A	B	O	E	N	A	C	T	I	S	F	V	U	P	E	R	J
Z	P	E	T	G	T	N	N	Y	M	Y	S	T	I	J	V	K	A	B	Y
K	J	H	T	G	R	C	P	O	V	K	T	P	Z	B	H	K	E	T	Y
H	X	I	H	H	I	D	Y	U	T	P	O	N	H	S	E	A	Z	T	J
A	W	C	G	E	O	L	B	H	D	T	N	I	C	H	C	L	E	Q	Z
R	D	D	O	N	F	V	V	P	O	Z	I	V	V	U	Y	J	I	D	T
R	R	Z	B	P	G	E	E	S	H	W	I	N	X	A	V	V	J	U	G
I	W	S	X	I	L	F	C	N	R	P	V	Q	C	J	V	K	I	G	S
S	L	S	W	F	T	A	H	A	Y	D	N	F	D	J	P	C	D	E	O
U	N	Q	C	B	O	D	N	F	G	Q	X	T	M	J	F	C	B	R	Y
H	R	O	T	H	O	S	T	D	G	R	O	F	E	D	R	Z	X	S	O
G	A	E	Y	X	U	U	T	V	X	G	J	T	J	A	Y	K	A	H	C
Y	V	R	L	I	C	M	L	E	M	O	Z	A	R	T	M	J	X	W	A
F	S	G	R	F	R	B	A	A	R	F	Z	S	O	U	S	A	H	I	J
X	X	L	E	I	U	X	N	N	N	B	E	R	N	S	T	E	I	N	V
H	R	A	E	A	M	P	L	J	N	G	L	K	N	Y	A	H	I	J	I
M	R	S	C	T	B	B	Z	A	D	M	E	W	A	R	D	O	Q	T	O
B	X	S	A	N	B	X	U	T	W	T	S	R	R	W	B	V	V	K	U
E	P	E	N	D	E	R	E	C	K	I	G	M	A	H	L	E	R	Y	S

1. HARRIS
2. MAHLER
3. COPLAND
4. SOUSA
5. GERSHWIN
6. WSCHUMANN
7. GLASS
8. GROFE
9. CRUMB
10. PENDERECKI
11. BOULANGER
12. FOSTER
13. MENOTTI
14. WARD
15. BERNSTEIN
16. PISTON
17. SIBELIUS
18. MOZART
19. BEETHOVEN
20. HAYDN

Classic Tunes & Tales
Composers Wordsearch No. 2
Answer Key

```
B J K A P M D S V R N P X L S G E L E N
V E Q A B O E N A C T I S F V U P E R J
Z P E T G T N N Y M Y S T I J V K A B Y
K J H T G R C P O V K T P Z B H K E T Y
H X I H H I D Y U T P O N H S E A Z T J
A W C G E O L B H D T N I C H C L E Q Z
R D D O N F V V P O Z I V V U Y J I D T
R R Z B P G E E S H W I N X A V V J U G
I W S X I L F C N R P V Q C J V K I G S
S L S W F T A H A Y D N F D J P C D E O
U N Q C B O D N F G Q X T M J F C B R Y
H R O T H O S T D G R O F E D R Z X S O
G A E Y X U U T V X G J T J A Y K A H C
Y V R L I C M L E M O Z A R T M J X W A
F S G R F R B A A R F Z S O U S A H I J
X X L E I U X N N N B E R N S T E I N V
H R A E A M P L J N G L K N Y A H I J I
M R S C T B B Z A D M E W A R D O Q T O
B X S A N B X U T W T S R R W B V V K U
E P E N D E R E C K I G M A H L E R Y S
```

1. HARRIS	2. MAHLER
3. COPLAND	4. SOUSA
5. GERSHWIN	6. WSCHUMANN
7. GLASS	8. GROFE
9. CRUMB	10. PENDERECKI
11. BOULANGER	12. FOSTER
13. MENOTTI	14. WARD
15. BERNSTEIN	16. PISTON
17. SIBELIUS	18. MOZART
19. BEETHOVEN	20. HAYDN

Classic Tunes & Tales
Composers Wordsearch No. 3

P	W	Q	O	H	V	N	Y	G	F	C	R	H	K	B	B	T	J	D	S
D	A	D	I	X	R	Q	D	Q	H	H	I	S	X	I	Q	B	H	A	C
P	S	C	S	I	J	O	U	Y	R	O	A	O	C	S	P	H	G	O	H
J	A	F	H	M	H	K	S	D	R	P	K	L	O	H	Z	X	T	V	U
C	Y	L	R	E	X	B	Q	S	Y	I	K	E	A	A	U	F	Q	T	B
U	C	X	E	P	L	F	F	H	I	N	N	G	M	X	Z	M	Z	F	E
G	I	C	T	S	Q	B	L	W	W	N	H	A	N	D	E	L	A	U	R
R	U	T	Q	N	T	B	E	D	Y	X	I	F	X	M	V	R	N	N	T
I	E	L	M	B	L	R	C	L	E	Q	Z	S	F	C	R	T	Y	E	N
E	K	B	Q	R	I	O	I	G	R	I	F	S	E	S	W	V	M	M	E
G	I	B	X	A	S	I	U	N	I	R	H	F	Z	N	P	B	F	A	Q
V	Q	A	W	H	Z	R	B	M	A	V	F	R	G	A	Z	N	A	S	S
H	E	F	W	M	T	I	E	I	T	Y	U	R	E	B	N	V	X	S	V
P	P	L	V	S	C	J	R	W	A	G	N	E	R	M	A	T	Q	E	G
C	Y	K	K	V	O	O	T	F	K	W	X	D	J	B	A	C	H	N	B
S	T	R	A	V	I	N	S	K	Y	G	E	D	U	A	M	U	U	E	W
E	V	I	V	A	L	D	I	Z	K	I	R	B	C	F	T	H	W	T	D
N	U	Z	X	E	W	P	A	K	K	X	O	P	E	X	A	Y	T	A	W
Y	T	O	P	Z	P	R	X	V	E	R	D	I	D	R	H	Y	F	D	C
I	B	G	M	M	W	C	C	M	F	R	E	S	C	O	B	A	L	D	I

1. PALESTRINA	2. STRAVINSKY
3. BACH	4. PACHELBEL
5. BRAHMS	6. SCHUBERT
7. RSCHUMANN	8. LISZT
9. WAGNER	10. GRIFFES
11. GRIEG	12. CHOPIN
13. VERDI	14. ROSSINI
15. MASSENET	16. VIVALDI
17. HANDEL	18. FRESCOBALDI
19. DUFAY	20. WEBER

Classic Tunes & Tales
Composers Wordsearch No. 3
Answer Key

```
P W Q O H V N Y G F C R H K B B T J D S
D A D I X R Q D Q H H I S X I Q B H A C
P S C S I J O U Y R O A O C S P H G O H
J A F H M H K S D R P K L O H Z X T V U
C Y L R E X B Q S Y I K E A A U F Q T B
U C X E P L F F H I N N G M X Z M Z F E
G I C T S Q B L W W N H A N D E L A U R
R U T Q N T B E D Y X I F X M V R N N T
I E L M B L R C L E Q Z S F C R T Y E N
E K B Q R I O G R I F S E S W V M M E
G I B X A S I U I R H F Z N P B F A Q
V Q A W H Z R B M A V F R G A Z N A S S
H E F W M T I E I T Y U R E B N V X S V
P P L V S C J R W A G N E R M A T Q E G
C Y K K V O O T F K W X D J B A C H N B
S T R A V I N S K Y G E D U A M U U E W
E V I V A L D I Z K I R B C F T H W T D
N U Z X E W P A K K X O P E X A Y T A W
Y T O P Z P R X V E R D I D R H Y F D C
I B G M M W C C M F R E S C O B A L D I
```

1. PALESTRINA	2. STRAVINSKY
3. BACH	4. PACHELBEL
5. BRAHMS	6. SCHUBERT
7. RSCHUMANN	8. LISZT
9. WAGNER	10. GRIFFES
11. GRIEG	12. CHOPIN
13. VERDI	14. ROSSINI
15. MASSENET	16. VIVALDI
17. HANDEL	18. FRESCOBALDI
19. DUFAY	20. WEBER

Classic Tunes Music Forms Wordsearch

R	S	J	L	W	C	V	B	O	Y	C	S	K	C	U	E	S	J	B	D
T	E	K	W	A	A	X	I	V	E	O	V	E	O	T	R	O	E	P	G
D	H	F	V	O	N	N	E	S	N	G	V	N	I	V	N	R	T	L	
O	E	E	R	V	O	O	A	R	Z	C	F	V	C	E	G	A	Z	Y	S
H	E	A	M	A	N	R	R	T	X	E	L	Y	E	L	N	T	O	G	Y
Q	F	Y	T	E	I	O	Y	U	W	R	D	K	R	R	F	A	W	X	M
P	I	H	R	W	A	N	K	R	U	T	M	O	T	A	A	I	D	P	P
R	Y	T	I	Y	E	N	R	E	V	O	M	M	O	V	N	I	B	E	H
E	M	Q	O	A	O	U	D	O	R	F	X	P	G	D	N	R	H	G	O
L	Y	P	M	O	O	U	W	V	N	Q	P	S	R	M	W	K	E	Z	N
C	A	N	T	A	T	A	T	M	A	D	D	S	O	E	Z	N	T	T	Y
D	I	T	R	B	A	O	D	P	H	R	O	O	S	F	L	G	Q	U	W
E	K	S	B	S	Y	K	E	W	F	Q	I	Q	S	D	J	U	B	C	X
D	Q	A	S	B	F	U	G	U	E	A	R	A	O	P	N	F	D	Q	N
A	S	R	B	S	U	Q	D	O	G	E	W	Z	T	T	A	Q	R	E	H
N	A	D	Q	S	Y	M	P	H	O	N	Y	D	W	I	D	Z	M	X	Y
E	A	U	Q	U	A	R	T	E	T	F	C	W	B	R	O	R	M	R	A
R	R	E	M	A	E	N	M	W	N	L	P	T	U	B	W	N	T	F	C
E	L	T	S	T	S	Y	M	O	R	A	T	O	R	I	O	Z	S	Q	R
S	E	L	L	A	Z	P	I	N	V	E	N	T	I	O	N	Q	X	U	Q

1. SONATA
2. THEMEANDVARIATIONS
3. SYMPHONY
4. CONCERTO
5. CONCERTOGROSSO
6. FUGUE
7. PRELUDE
8. REFRAIN
9. RONDO
10. SERENADE
11. TERNARY
12. BINARY
13. OVERTURE
14. INVENTION
15. CANTATA
16. ORATORIO
17. DUET
18. TRIO
19. QUARTET
20. CANON

Classic Tunes Music Forms
Wordsearch
Answer Key

```
R S J L W C V B O Y C S K C U E S J B D
T E K W A A X I V E O V E O T R O E P G
D H F V O N N N E S N G V N I V N R T L
O E E R V O O A R Z C F V C E G A Z Y W
H E A M A N R R T X E L Y E L N T O G F
Q F Y T E I O Y U W R D K R R F A W X E
P I H R W A N K R U T M O T A A I D P H
R Y T I Y E N R E V O M M O V N I B E O
E M Q O A O U D O R F X P G D N R H G A
L Y P M O O U W V N Q P S R M W K E Z U
C A N T A T A T M A D D S O E Z N T T R
D I T R B A O D P H R O O S F L G Q U W
E K S B S Y K E W F Q I Q S D J U B C X
D Q A S B F U G U E A R A O P N F D Q N
A S R B S U Q D O G E W Z T T A Q R E H
N A D Q S Y M P H O N Y D W I D Z M X Y
E A U Q U A R T E T F C W B R O R M R A
R R E M A E N M W N L P T U B W N T F C
E L T S T S Y M O R A T O R I O Z S Q R
S E L L A Z P I N V E N T I O N Q X U Q
```

1. SONATA	2. THEMEANDVARIATIONS
3. SYMPHONY	4. CONCERTO
5. CONCERTOGROSSO	6. FUGUE
7. PRELUDE	8. REFRAIN
9. RONDO	10. SERENADE
11. TERNARY	12. BINARY
13. OVERTURE	14. INVENTION
15. CANTATA	16. ORATORIO
17. DUET	18. TRIO
19. QUARTET	20. CANON

Classic Tunes Instruments
Wordsearch

V	K	P	I	C	C	O	L	O	Q	I	S	B	W	N	A	A	P	N	J
Q	I	O	C	I	T	T	S	M	F	D	N	A	Q	V	C	E	I	S	F
H	N	H	E	P	V	E	R	J	X	I	A	L	S	S	O	R	A	X	E
J	A	W	U	L	Y	N	G	Q	X	O	R	A	X	Q	N	O	N	F	N
T	M	R	N	E	U	I	F	H	Q	P	E	L	M	Y	O	P	O	M	O
T	C	L	P	I	L	R	Y	O	K	H	D	A	E	U	W	H	B	W	H
T	T	W	C	S	W	A	R	Z	E	O	R	I	P	S	C	O	Z	Z	P
C	R	O	G	X	I	L	P	W	K	N	U	K	U	F	Y	N	A	B	O
W	U	O	K	A	K	C	T	M	P	E	M	A	R	N	U	E	H	E	X
S	M	E	L	S	T	Z	H	N	R	D	R	M	Q	F	C	T	A	A	A
A	P	B	M	U	R	L	Z	O	L	P	Z	Z	K	T	U	Y	Y	P	S
O	E	I	H	E	O	P	O	I	R	A	C	C	O	R	D	I	O	N	X
X	T	G	O	U	F	G	C	I	W	D	K	K	A	N	K	L	U	N	G
T	R	O	M	B	O	N	E	D	C	L	A	R	Y	N	E	T	A	N	T
C	H	O	R	D	O	P	H	O	N	E	O	W	F	O	B	O	W	O	Y
Z	I	T	H	E	R	L	Z	O	U	B	P	B	J	L	T	R	Z	X	C
M	E	M	B	R	A	N	O	P	H	O	N	E	O	A	G	O	I	L	O
L	X	V	V	U	U	E	J	G	Z	T	Q	C	P	E	F	C	A	M	M
Y	T	G	X	Q	F	C	F	D	O	U	M	D	H	Y	H	V	E	R	F
S	J	Q	S	A	X	O	F	I	F	E	E	Y	C	I	L	I	S	O	A

1. PIANO
2. PICCOLO
3. TRUMPET
4. CLARINET
5. TROMBONE
6. OBOE
7. SAXOPHONE
8. VIHUELA
9. IDIOPHONE
10. CHORDOPHONE
11. KYOTO
12. ZITHER
13. MEMBRANOPHONE
14. AEROPHONE
15. ANKLUNG
16. SNAREDRUM
17. FIFE
18. ACCORDION
19. HARPSICHORD
20. BALALAIKA

Classic Tunes Instruments
Wordsearch
Answer Key

V	K	P	I	C	C	O	L	O	Q	I	S	B	W	N	A	A	P	N	J
Q	I	O	C	I	T	T	S	M	F	D	N	A	Q	V	C	E	I	S	F
H	N	H	E	P	V	E	R	J	X	I	A	L	S	S	O	R	A	X	E
J	A	W	U	L	Y	N	G	Q	X	O	R	A	X	Q	N	O	N	F	N
T	M	R	N	E	U	I	F	H	Q	P	E	L	M	Y	O	P	O	M	O
T	C	L	P	I	L	R	Y	O	K	H	D	A	E	U	W	H	B	W	H
T	T	W	C	S	W	A	R	Z	E	O	R	I	P	S	C	O	Z	Z	P
C	R	O	G	X	I	L	P	W	K	N	U	K	U	F	Y	N	A	B	O
W	U	O	K	A	K	C	T	M	P	E	M	A	R	N	U	E	H	E	X
S	M	E	L	S	T	Z	H	N	R	D	R	M	Q	F	C	T	A	A	A
A	P	B	M	U	R	L	Z	O	L	P	Z	Z	K	T	U	Y	Y	P	S
O	E	I	H	E	O	P	O	I	R	A	C	C	O	R	D	I	O	N	X
X	T	G	O	U	F	G	C	I	W	D	K	K	A	N	K	L	U	N	G
T	R	O	M	B	O	N	E	D	C	L	A	R	Y	N	E	T	A	N	T
C	H	O	R	D	O	P	H	O	N	E	O	W	F	O	B	O	W	O	Y
Z	I	T	H	E	R	L	Z	O	U	B	P	B	J	L	T	R	Z	X	C
M	E	M	B	R	A	N	O	P	H	O	N	E	O	A	G	O	I	L	O
L	X	V	V	U	U	E	J	G	Z	T	Q	C	P	E	F	C	A	M	M
Y	T	G	X	Q	F	C	F	D	O	U	M	D	H	Y	H	V	E	R	F
S	J	Q	S	A	X	O	F	I	F	E	E	Y	C	I	L	I	S	O	A

1. PIANO	2. PICCOLO
3. TRUMPET	4. CLARINET
5. TROMBONE	6. OBOE
7. SAXOPHONE	8. VIHUELA
9. IDIOPHONE	10. CHORDOPHONE
11. KYOTO	12. ZITHER
13. MEMBRANOPHONE	14. AEROPHONE
15. ANKLUNG	16. SNAREDRUM
17. FIFE	18. ACCORDION
19. HARPSICHORD	20. BALALAIKA

Musical Terms & Symbols Wordsearch

```
T D C F S M A J O R G D D T W S E X T E T R B N H
Q O T A R E D O M Y H O E A D U O G R A L O X L G
V B A S S C L E F V T O L C A S U P R N I Q O F A
C B L F J M X O H T G L N J R C O E H E O V M O O
H A Z V T Z R I E E P H A O E C C D F L I I M V
R K P D A T S R E G C Q V A I D S E T O I R S I I
Z I C M S V G C R Z J N G S R P N C N E M T S S C
T E T E K E M O I K C T A L W M I E E T T U I S V
R K A A L H X T E M E Q J S T H O T C N Z O T I A
E M G L R C F R G T A X S K S O P N C S D S R N L
B G A L C D I R N F X N N Z I I E S Y H E O O A I
L J O L A C A I A L R A Y G Z M A V D P L R F I R
E O L A L N U N R P T N A D E B L N T R D D C P O
C Y Q Y F Q O R D U R D T Z Y A A E E O O S M C T
L W R L E C Z T R O A J Z T N M T R T R F H H P C
E L F A R I B A A D L O W O D P O A O R L N C O U
F E B C M T L V Z C F E T S J R V D R Q I K Z N D
C G X I A N H C A O L R H B N X L A E O U A A A N
P A S S T A P R R V D Y E S A R H P W R N E D I O
I T L S A M A T E M P O D R M W J V A H N I X P C
J O J A E O E T L V I A N D A N T E P B N P M O T
H T X L S R O Q U W M R J H N S T A C C A T O Z A
Q T O C T N A F A E T R O F G J C T R V G J V Z L
A T B K E T I G X R D E S E J R E F O P Q J V E F
N E P R A H S B D V D I W W I Q D S M O R Q V M F
```

RANGE	ADAGIO	ALLEGRO	ALLEGRETTO
ANDANTE	BASSCLEF	TREBLECLEF	FERMATA
CRESCENDO	DECRESCENDO	CONDUCTOR	RENAISSANCE
BAROQUE	CLASSICAL	ROMANTIC	MODERN
PITCH	LARGO	MODERATO	SHARP
FLAT	NATURAL	STACCATO	ACCENT
LEGATO	PHRASE	VIRTUOSO	MAJOR
MINOR	MODE	TONAL	ATONAL
CHORDS	HARMONY	RITARDANDO	ATEMPO
DYNAMICS	FORTE	PIANO	MEZZOPIANO
MEZZOFORTE	FORTISSIMO	PIANISSIMO	MAESTRO
TWELVETONE	SEXTET	SEPTET	OCTET
QUINTET	TRIAD		

Musical Terms & Symbols Wordsearch
Answer Key

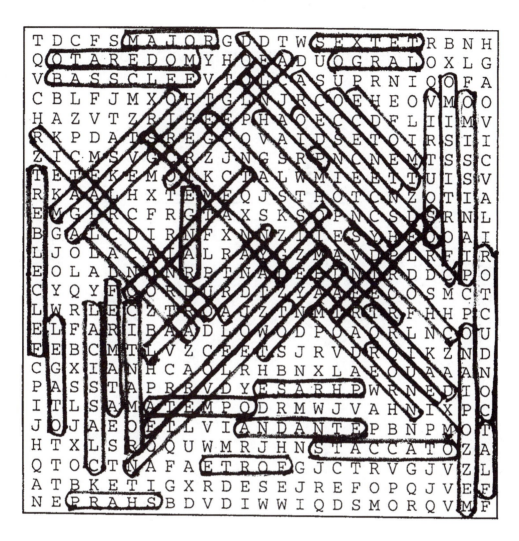

RANGE	ADAGIO	ALLEGRO	ALLEGRETTO
ANDANTE	BASSCLEF	TREBLECLEF	FERMATA
CRESCENDO	DECRESCENDO	CONDUCTOR	RENAISSANCE
BAROQUE	CLASSICAL	ROMANTIC	MODERN
PITCH	LARGO	MODERATO	SHARP
FLAT	NATURAL	STACCATO	ACCENT
LEGATO	PHRASE	VIRTUOSO	MAJOR
MINOR	MODE	TONAL	ATONAL
CHORDS	HARMONY	RITARDANDO	ATEMPO
DYNAMICS	FORTE	PIANO	MEZZOPIANO
MEZZOFORTE	FORTISSIMO	PIANISSIMO	MAESTRO
TWELVETONE	SEXTET	SEPTET	OCTET
QUINTET	TRIAD		

Decorate and Color Page
(Notes)

Decorate the snowman with 𝅗𝅥 or 𝅘𝅥.

Decorate and Color Page
(Notes and Symbols)

Decorate the sailboat with music notes and symbols.

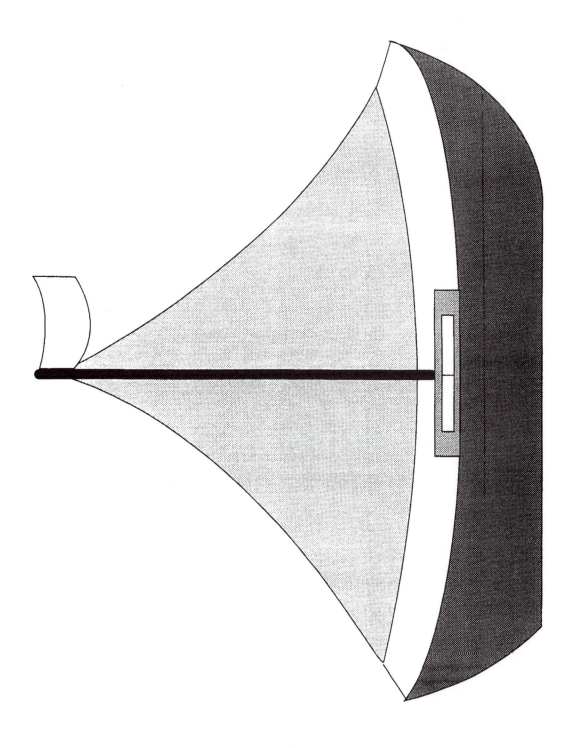

Dot-to-Dot Color Page

Connect the dots 1 to 20 and A-B, C-D, E-F, G-H, I-J

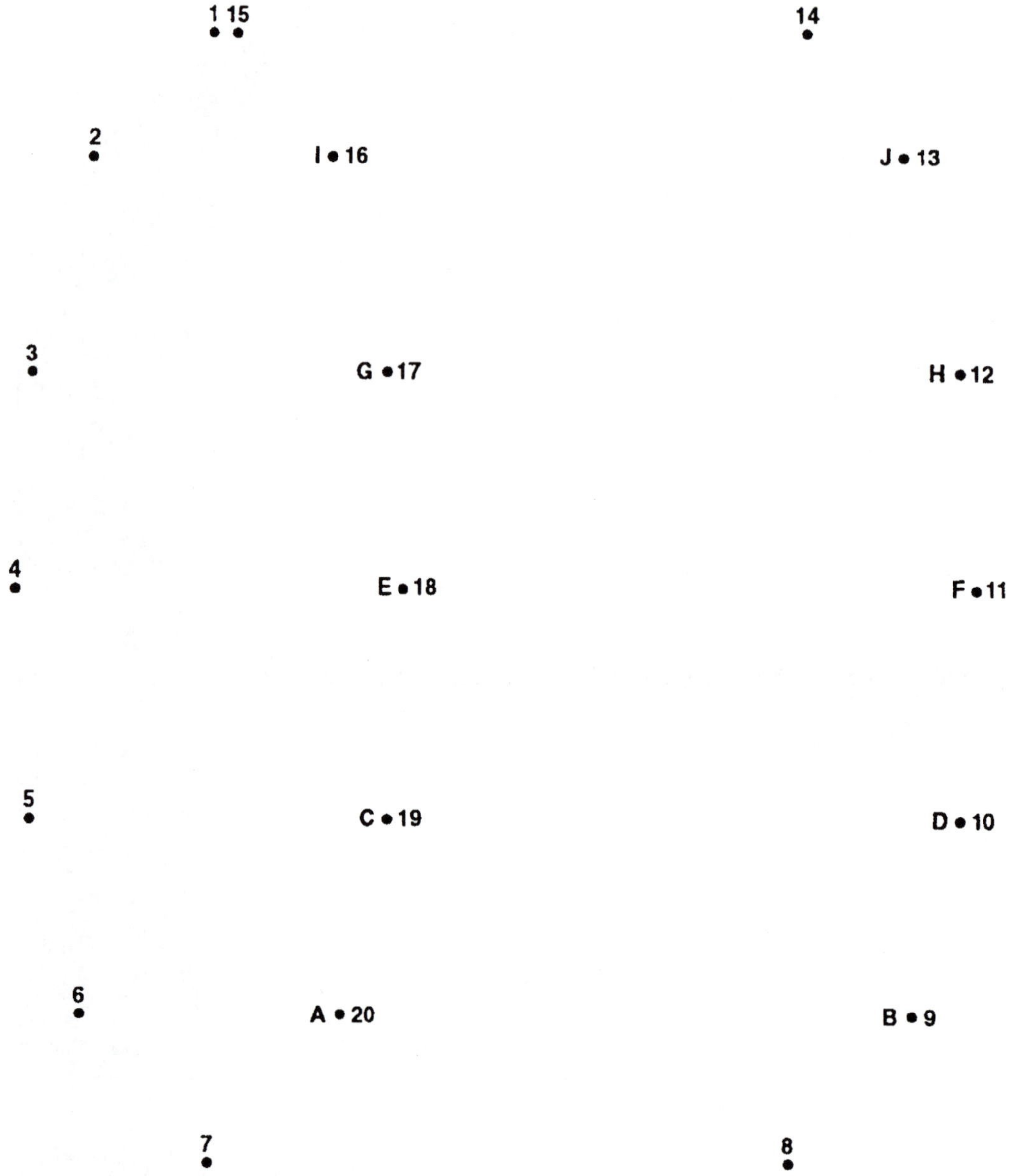

1 15

14

2

I • 16

J • 13

3

G • 17

H • 12

4

E • 18

F • 11

© 1997 by Parker Publishing Company

5

C • 19

D • 10

6

A • 20

B • 9

7

8

Classic Tunes & Tales
Historical Timeline

Events	Date	People	Period
	1400	Columbus	Renaissance
Discovery		Da Vinci	
of	1525	Michelangelo	
America		Palestrina	
		Galileo	
Gutenberg	1678	Newton	
printing press		first opera	
Mayflower		Pocahontas	
The 13 original	1685	Vivaldi	Baroque
colonies est.		Bach/Handel	
		Rococo	
	1732	Haydn	
Industrial		The Symphony	
Revolution			
	1750	Mozart	Classical
Declaration		Beethoven	
of	1811	Liszt	
Independence		Verdi/Wagner	Romantic
		Dickens	
War of 1812		Victor Hugo/Hunchback	
	1856		
Civil War			
	1898	Debussy/Impressionist	Modern/Contemporary
		Monet	
		Gershwin	
Alamo	1905	Copland	
World War I		W. Schumann	
Great Depression	1920		
World War II		Zwilich	
Vietnam		Adams	
Gulf War	1990	Electronic music	

337

Classic Tunes Bulletin Board Plans

1. *Composers and Their Music* (Display #1)

   Take 9 x 12 construction paper and fold it in half. Place the tune title, composer, or a tune story of a Classic Tune on the outside. Put the composer, title, or story that is appropriate and the corresponding answer to each one. Students can walk by the bulletin board and review or learn about the classics.

2. *Symbols in Music* (Display #2)

   Use file cards and file card pockets. Put the music symbol on a pocket and numerous symbol cards in the symbol name pockets. Put the symbols on one side of the bulletin board and the symbol names on the other. Allow students to place the symbol cards in the symbol card pockets.

3. *Fifth Graders Writing About Mozart* (Display #3)

   This board can use any other grade level doing the appropriate assignment. Use the various tune activities that involve writing to display student work.

4. *Music Taking Form* (Display #4)

   Put the scheme of a music form on one side of the board and the name of the form on the other. Make copies of the board so the students can try to figure out the forms on their own. Use one envelope with the blank forms and the other for a place to put the filled-out forms returned by the students.

5. *Who Composed This?* (Display #5)

   Make twelve to fifteen 2×10-inch oaktag cards. Put the titles of the Classic Tunes on one side and their composers on the other. Punch a hole in the upper middle part of each card, and tie a piece of string or yarn through the hole. Tack the card on the board so students can turn the card over for the answers.

6. *Music in History* (Display #6)

   Make three columns on the board. The column headings should be Period, Event/People, and Composer. Under the Period heading, put Renaissance, Baroque, Classical, Romantic, and Modern (Contemporary, Impressionist, if possible). Add the historical events and people and the correct column and period. Create an envelope with composer names inside. Use empty envelopes under each period. Allow students to place the composers with their corresponding time periods.

7. *Composers Around the World* (Display #7)

   Put a map of the world on the board. Either write the names of composers on their countries or make composer name cards so the students can place them at the appropriate countries or cities.

8. *Who's Who?* (Display #8)

   Attach the various composer portraits on one side (or section) of the board and their names, in random-order, on the other side. Students can guess who's who.

   Alternative: Use biographical information instead of a portrait.

Bulletin Board Displays

1

Composers and Their Music

Name the composer	Name the tune	What's the story?
Eine	Bach	Shot an apple
Trout	Rimsky-Korsakoff	Ghost of
Liebestraum	Tchaikovsky	Swan swim
Water Music	Chopin	Hunchback

2

Symbols in Music

Symbols

Name

Staccato Fermata

Legato Treble Clef

Tie Sharp

Bass Clef Accent

3

Fifth Graders Writing About Mozart

4

Music Taking Form

Symbols

A B A
A B A C A

A B

Match the form and its name. Take a form and fill it out.

Name
Fugue
Theme and Variations
Ternary (3-part)
Rondo
Binary (2-part)

Bulletin Board Displays

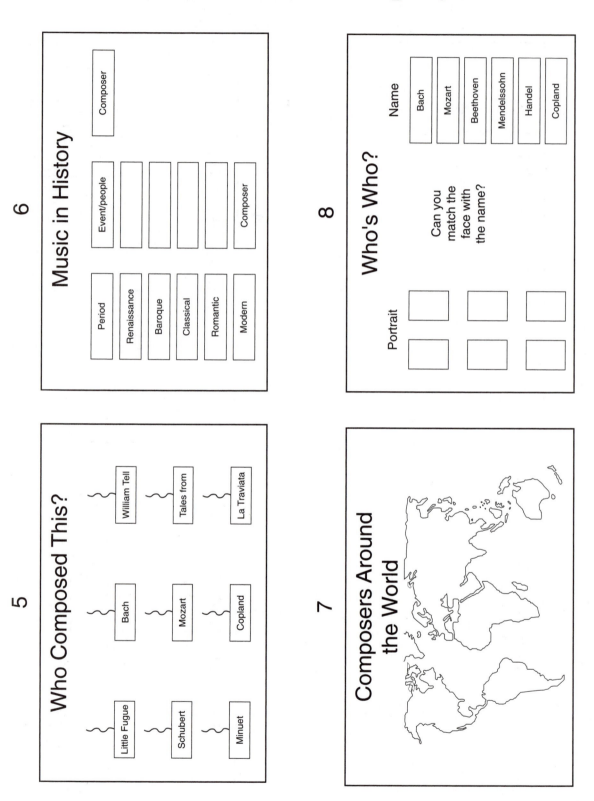

6

Music in History

Period	Event/people	Composer
Renaissance		
Baroque		
Classical		
Romantic		
Modern		Composer

5

Who Composed This?

Little Fugue ∼ Bach ∼ William Tell

Schubert ∼ Mozart ∼ Tales from

Minuet ∼ Copland ∼ La Traviata

8

Who's Who?

Portrait

Can you match the face with the name?

Name

Bach
Mozart
Beethoven
Mendelssohn
Handel
Copland

7

Composers Around the World

340

Classic Tunes & Tales
Lesson Objectives/Reference Page

Levels	Symbols	Repeats	Articulation	Dynamic	Periods	Rhythm	Opera	Terms	Form
I	Fire Bird Surprise Don Giovanni	Bolero Grand Can	Surprise Fire Bird Swan Lake Peer Gynt	Suprise	Baroque Classical Romantic Modern	All	William Tell Don Giovanni	Adagio William Tell Eine Kleine Peer Gynt	William Tell Minuet Swan Lake Fire Bird
II	5th Symphony Symphony No. 2 Fant-Imp	Trumpet Vol Happy Farmer Symphony No. 2 Canon Rodeo	Trumpet Vol Trout Symphony No. 2 Rodeo Fant-Imp Largo	Largo Concerto Sym Fan	Baroque Classical Romantic Modern	All		Symphony No. 2 Largo	Canon Nutcracker Rodeo
III	Stars & Stripes Scheherazade Till		Rigoletto Can Can Stars & Stripes Scheherazade Till Sym Fant		Baroque Romantic	All	Rigoletto Toreador	Rour Seasons Rigoletto Can Can Concerto Symph Fant	Hallelujah
IV	Rhapsody Minuet Barber		Il Trov Aida		Baroque Classical Modern	All	Barber Wedding Ch Il Trovatore Aida	Emp Str Quartet Finlandia Wedding Ch Il Trovatore Symp No. 40	Little Fugue Emp Str Quartet Rhapsody Minuet Aida
V	Meditation Vienna W Unfin Symph La Traviata	Liebestraum Water Music La Traviata	La Gioconda Meditation Vienna Woods Water Music	Moldau	Baroque Romantic Modern	All	La Gioconda Meditation	Moldau Water Music La Traviata	Liebestraum Water Music Grand Can

Teacher Notes

Teacher Notes

Teacher Notes

Teacher Notes

Teacher Notes

Teacher Notes

Teacher Notes